DAILY LIFE OF

THE NEW AMERICANS

Recent Titles in
The Greenwood Press Daily Life Through History Series

DAILY LIFE OF

THE NEW AMERICANS

Immigration since 1965

CHRISTOPH STROBEL

The Greenwood Press Daily Life Through History Series

 GREENWOOD

AN IMPRINT OF ABC-CLIO, LLC
Santa Barbara, California • Denver, Colorado • Oxford, England

Library of Congress Cataloging-in-Publication Data

Strobel, Christoph.
    Daily life of the new Americans : immigration since 1965 / Christoph Strobel.
        p. cm. — (The Greenwood Press Daily life through history series)
    Includes bibliographical references and index.
    ISBN 978–0–313–36313–9 (hard copy : alk. paper) — ISBN 978–0–313–36314–6 (ebook)
1. Immigrants—United States—Social life and customs—20th century.   2. Immigrants—United States—Social life and customs—21st century.   3. Immigrants—United States—Social conditions.   4. Immigrants—United States—Biography.   5. Minorities—United States—Social life and customs.   6. Minorities—United States—Social conditions.
7. United States—Emigration and immigration—History—20th century.   8. United States—Emigration and immigration—History—21st century.   I. Title.
JV6455.S95   2010
305.9′069120973—dc22   2010000437

ISBN: 978–0–313–36313–9
EISBN: 978–0–313–36314–6

14 13 12 11 10   1 2 3 4 5

This book is also available on the World Wide Web as an eBook.
Visit www.abc-clio.com for details.

Greenwood
An Imprint of ABC-CLIO, LLC

ABC-CLIO, LLC
130 Cremona Drive, P.O. Box 1911
Santa Barbara, California 93116-1911

This book is printed on acid-free paper ∞

Manufactured in the United States of America

CONTENTS

PREFACE

Since the 1960s, a growing number of immigrants from all corners of the globe have arrived in America. This trend has dramatically transformed the face of the modern United States. U.S. Census data from 1970 indicate that only 4.7 percent of America's populace in that year was foreign born. By 2000, however, the percentage of the population born outside the United States rose to about 11 percent. Since then, more immigrants have continued to arrive, and the percentage is likely to rise even further.

This is not the first time in history that the United States experienced a high influx of immigrants. The nineteenth and the early twentieth century saw a major wave of migrants come to America—many to start a fresh life in their newly adopted country. In the first decade of the twentieth century, the foreign-born population in the United States reached an estimated peak of almost 15 percent. Two previous volumes in Greenwood's *Daily Life Through History Series* have addressed the history and the experiences of these earlier immigrants. James Bergquist's *Daily Life in Immigrant America, 1820–1870* examines the "first wave," and June Granatir Alexander's *Daily Life in Immigrant America, 1870–1920* reviews the "second wave" of immigration to the United States.

Immigration seems to be on the minds of everybody in the United States today. The media, politicians, businessmen, community leaders, academics, pundits, and ordinary Americans are debating the political, economic, social, and cultural ramifications that the new wave of global immigrants is having on the country. Given the timeliness of the subject, it is not surprising that scholars have focused significant attention on the new wave of immigration sweeping the United States. Much of the scholarly literature, published in the form of books and academic papers, is highly specialized and loaded with jargon. It often focuses on the lives of a single immigrant group or on the experiences of various immigrant groups living in a single community. Only a few studies take a national perspective, and most of these books are geared toward researchers, graduate students, and advanced college students in upper-level classes. What is missing is a scholarly yet accessible narrative reference history of the daily life of the recent wave of immigrants that is not only geared toward academics, teachers, and instructors, but also toward college and high school students as well as general readers. This book hopes to fill this void.

The volume is organized in a thematic way, underscoring the various themes of daily life among immigrants since the passage of the Immigration and Nationality Act of 1965. Each chapter of the book underscores the diversity and complexity of the newcomers' experience. Chapter 1 examines the various and diverse migration stories. Why and how do immigrants come to America, and what are their perceptions of the United States? Chapter 2 looks at the immigrants' economic life. What are their jobs, and in what economic enterprises do they participate? Chapter 3 scrutinizes the family life of immigrants and looks at identity, family relations, and intergenerational issues. Chapter 4 examines the community life and culture of immigrants as well as their interactions with mainstream society. It examines such issues as religion, places of worship, ethnic organizations, social networks, and festivals. Chapter 5 analyzes the stereotypes and discrimination that immigrants face, and it also explores some of the tensions that exist within and between immigrant communities. Chapter 6 examines the role that politics and policy plays in the daily life of immigrants.

My experience as an immigrant to this country has also shaped my perspective and interest in the history of international immigration. It has led me to study the trends and tendencies of this phenomenon in American and world history.

While working on this project, I benefited from the help of many people. The book draws from the work of a large community of scholars, who are cited and acknowledged in the endnotes and mostly in the bibliography of this book. Thanks to the Interlibrary Loan Department at my home institution, the University of Massachusetts Lowell, for providing me with numerous requests for books and articles. My editor at ABC-CLIO, Mariah Gumpert, has given me valuable suggestions and feedback. Here at UMass Lowell, I also benefited from the help, suggestions, or assistance of several colleagues. Michael Pierson provided valuable comments and continued encouragement. My chair, Joseph Lipchitz, came through with requests for supplies and, more importantly, he accommodated my teaching schedule requests, which enabled me to find time to work on the manuscript. Discussions with my colleagues Shehong Chen, Bob Forrant,

Chad Montrie, and Susan Thomson on immigration also proved insightful. Janette Marquez provided valuable administrative assistance on several occasions.

I am grateful to several people who have shared their oral histories with me in interviews and discussions. These conversations have helped to shape my understanding of the rich diversity and complexity of the immigrant experience in the United States. Besides telling me their stories, several immigrants were gracious to invite me to their places of worship, cultural associations, and various festivals.

I have benefited from the help of many of my students. Teaching at UMass Lowell is a constant reminder of the importance of the recent history of international migration to the United States. Every semester I teach a significant number of undergraduates who are of Latino, Indian, Southeast Asian, Brazilian, African, Pakistani, Middle Eastern, and Chinese background. These "immigrant students" sit alongside their "mainstream" American peers whose Irish, German, Italian, Greek, Slavic, Franco-Canadian, and Scandinavian names reveal the only slightly more distant immigrant history of their own families.

Over the years, several of my students have served as my cultural brokers and teachers. They have taught me many lessons and have patiently answered my questions about their cultures, customs, and traditions. They provided—and still provide me with—valuable insights, helped me to make connections in their communities, and at times volunteered to share their stories. Many probably do not realize how much a professor can learn from his undergraduates.

Shaped by the processes of global migration and globalization, and similar to many places in the United States, the world has come to the city where I work and where I've lived for almost four years. Buddhist and Hindu temples, mosques, churches, and immigrant stores and restaurants that cater to Southeast Asian, Latino, Brazilian, Indian, and African customers are scattered throughout the city. Having moved recently to an area suburb, living about a mile outside of Lowell, the changing face of America is apparent in this community as well. There is an Islamic Center close by, a Buddhist temple, several immigrant-run businesses, and various foreign-born residents who live in my neighborhood. The changes brought on by immigration have become part of the mosaic and have helped to alter the face of the United States.

As always, my wife Kristin was a great support. Kristin patiently read and commented on drafts and asked many important questions about the project. She patiently listened to my ramblings about issues of conceptualization and organization related to this book. Kristin always gave valuable feedback. This book is dedicated to her and our daughter Lora.

INTRODUCTION

The new wave of immigration into the United States that began in the mid-1960s and accelerated in the 1990s and early twenty-first century has changed the face of America dramatically, as the United States has inarguably become a more diverse place during the last few decades. European immigration has declined and has been vastly overtaken by a population influx stemming from the non-Western world, with people arriving from Latin America, Asia, Africa, and the Middle East. Immigration to the United States has truly become a global pursuit.

Between 1971 and 2000, 19.9 million legal migrants have entered the United States. Millions more who arrived were undocumented. The number of new arrivals during the last quarter of the twentieth century significantly outnumbered the 18.2 million immigrants who entered the United States between 1891 and 1920—a peak period of immigration in the nation's history. From 2000 to 2005, nearly 8 million immigrants arrived—the current record for a five-year period in American immigration history.

Consequently, the number of foreign-born residents in the United States has increased nearly fourfold from 9.7 million in 1960 to 35.2 million in 2005. In terms of percentage, this figure puts the foreign-born population in the early twenty-first century at 12.1 percent of the overall U.S. population. While these numbers are impressive, this period is not the historic high point, which was reached in the early decades of the twentieth century at 14.7 percent.

The recent wave of immigration is part of a worldwide trend. Experts approximate that, globally speaking, one person out of 35 is an international migrant. In 2002, an estimated 175 million people were living in a country that was not the place of their birth. With approximately 35 million immigrants, the United States is the largest receiver country, followed by Russia at 13.3 million and Germany at 7.3 million. International migration is thus playing a critical role in global political, economic, social, and cultural development. It is part of a worldwide phenomenon.[1]

THE UNITED STATES AND IMMIGRATION

Why was the rate of immigration so high in the early as well as the late twentieth century, but lower in the middle of the century? Much of it had to do with the government's approach toward immigration. The U.S. immigration policy underwent significant changes in the early decades of the twentieth century, following a comparatively more open immigration policy of the nineteenth century. Spurred by a wave of nativism and anti-immigrant sentiment, the nation dramatically decreased its acceptance of foreigners. This shift was especially exemplified by the passage of the Immigration Act of 1924.

This law, which imposed quotas for immigrants from each country based on the census numbers from the 1890s, favored established immigrant groups from western and northern Europe and made it particularly hard for eastern and southern Europeans to settle in the United States. Furthermore, the Immigration Act excluded Asians almost entirely. Thus, for several decades the foreign-born population of the United States declined.

During the last few decades, immigration has once again become a central social phenomenon in the United States. The Immigration and Nationality Act of 1965, which abolished the national origin quotas and lifted restrictions by liberalizing immigration from Asia, has spurred a new wave of people coming into this country. Unlike the nineteenth century and early twentieth century, when immigrants predominantly came from Europe, the vast majority of today's newcomers originate from Latin America, Asia, the Middle East, and Africa.

While it has become something of cliché today, the world truly has come to the United States. Despite the dramatic diversity and cultural differences that exist among the global immigrants that come to the United States, there are also similarities. Due to the global reach of the U.S. media and entertainment industries and the processes that we generalize today as "globalization," newcomers to the United States, no matter what their background, often have at least some familiarity with American culture.

Immigration has its opponents, and this opposition came to the forefront with the terrorist attacks on the United States that occurred on September 11, 2001. These horrible events were accompanied by a growing wave of xenophobia, which spurred an insular mood among at least some Americans. As a result, immigration became a hot-button issue in several election campaigns in the first decade of this millennium. Yet, in many ways the debate over immigration was already being waged before the events of September 11.

In fact, strong anti-immigrant sentiment has been part of the American political discourse since the days of the early republic. Then, as now, many Americans felt that the United States was becoming overcrowded and that immigration was harmful to the economy. They believed it threatened America's culture through outside influences and that immigrants took jobs from Americans or depressed wages. Although the focus of today's debate is on "illegal" immigration, the bigoted and sometimes racist images raised by the disputes have a negative impact on mainstream society's perception of all immigrants. The heatedness of the political discourse in recent years leads many policy experts to believe that dramatic political changes could occur and that such developments could potentially curtail immigration to the United States in the future.

Partly due to the recent wave of immigration, the United States now ranks among the most ethnically and racially diverse nations on Earth. As the newcomers are becoming part of the diverse American mosaic, they are also helping to change and enrich the United States. As immigrants recreate their lives in their new surroundings, they bring with them their cultural norms and understandings, religions, food, languages, and other aspects that shape their daily life.

Thus, just like the European immigrants at the turn of the last century, this generation of immigrants is transforming the United States. Furthermore, the newcomers are being changed by this country through a variety of complex and diverse processes—they are adopting and embracing American values, norms, culture, and practices. A better understanding of their experience can illuminate and improve our understanding of our changing society.

The large presence of immigrants in America raises a variety of questions. How does the wave of global migrants impact America? How are they seen and treated by Americans? What are the forces that led them to leave their native country and come to America? What are the international and transnational implications of immigration? What issues and challenges do immigrants and their children face in the United States? What sort of lives do immigrants lead?

THE CHANGING FACE OF AMERICA

Immigration is helping to change the face of America. According to census data, Latinos have overtaken African Americans as the largest minority group in the United States. This expansion is largely due to the increase in immigration in the last few decades. In addition, it is estimated that about one in five children in American schools is either foreign born or the child of an immigrant, a development that certainly has consequences for the education system in this country.

Historically, immigration was largely an urban phenomenon that influenced major gateway cities in the United States. This trend continues today, as immigration is centered in cities like New York, Los Angeles, Houston, Chicago, and Miami, communities that have been major receiving areas for immigrants. Furthermore, about 67 percent of immigrants live in only six states: California, Florida, Illinois, New Jersey, New York, and Texas. However, recent immigration is not only a localized phenomenon confined to a few limited urban areas and states. Its impact can be felt nationally, not only in big cities but also in many suburbs, small towns, and even rural areas all across America. According to *The Economist* magazine, "This is producing some of the most dramatic demographic changes in recent American history."

Immigration is now extending its reach to rural and urban areas of the South, West, and Midwest, specifically to states such as North Carolina, Georgia, Arkansas, Utah, Tennessee, and Nebraska that traditionally did not experience much of an influx of immigrants. Today these areas are attracting newcomers who in many instances are lured by jobs in the meat-packing and food-processing industries, and these newcomers are changing the racial and ethnic make up of these regions. From 1990 to 2000 alone, for example, the immigrant population of North Carolina increased 274 percent and Georgia's grew 233 percent.

These numbers reveal only a small part of the story. In fact, immigration is having a dramatic impact on American society, as it changes the social and cultural landscape of the United States. The arrival of large numbers of newcomers influences local labor and housing markets as well as the social infrastructures in hospitals and schools.

Immigrants bring with them their ways of life and their cultures. These new arrivals open up restaurants and stores that cater to their fellow immigrants' tastes in food, clothing, and entertainment, but they are also frequented by some mainstream American customers.

Newcomers join American churches (often revitalizing struggling religious communities) or open up new places of worship that cater to their own specific spiritual needs. They bring with them their sports as well, as evidenced in many public parks where immigrants can be seen playing pick-up games of soccer or cricket, and they celebrate their traditional festivals in their new surroundings. Many continue to listen to their native country's music and watch soap operas and other television shows aired in their native languages, which are broadcast by satellite television or through ethnic media based in the United States. Many also continue to maintain close relationships with their communities of origin, traveling back and forth, providing financial support to family members, or sending their children to their home countries to be raised by their grandparents or other close relatives.[2]

Immigrant-themed art. Scott Olson/Getty Images.

THE EMERGENCE OF NEW IDENTITIES

This book provides an introduction to the daily life of immigrants who have come to the United States since 1965. It is by no means a comprehensive account. Instead, it attempts to provide a glimpse of the main trends, trajectories, tendencies, and patterns that shape the diverse lives of immigrants.

Immigration has led to the preservation, creation, and reinvention of traditions, ways of life, customs, and practices among the newcomer populations in the United States. Simultaneously, immigrants are being changed by their experiences in this country as they adopt certain aspects of American culture, practices, and values. As they shape and, in turn, are shaped by the United States in significant ways, they are developing new identities. These are complex, diverse, and nuanced processes in which immigrants develop hybrid identities as "ethnic" or hyphen-Americans and, at the same time, emphasize their own ethnic, national, social, and racial identities and backgrounds.

This does not mean that immigrant communities are homogenous groups. In fact, there often exist significant class, cultural, and racial diversity within specific groups.

At the same time, identities are also defined by outsiders. Immigrants are often perceived as different or as "others" by mainstream American society. Their skin color, accent, mannerisms, culture, and customs often differentiate them—sometimes to a point where they feel ostracized by the larger community that surrounds them. Due to such pressures and perceptions, many immigrants believe that they will be identified always as different, even as they try to make a new life for themselves and their families in the United States and also attempt to blend into American society in many ways.

NOTES

1. Mary Waters and Reed Ueda, "Introduction," in *The New Americans: A Guide to Immigration Since 1965* (Cambridge, MA: Harvard University Press, 2007), 2–3; Stephen Castles and Mark Miller, *The Age of Migration: International Population Movements in the Modern World.* Third Edition (New York, NY: Guilford Press, 2003), X.

2. "Immigrants Are Transforming Some Surprising Parts of America," *The Economist*, February 23–29, 2008, 46.

CHRONOLOGY

1882	The Chinese Exclusion Act is developed.
1892	The Geary Act, which initially extended the Chinese Exclusion Act by 10 years, is developed. Congress made it a permanent law in 1902 and also required persons of Chinese origin to carry certificates of residence.
1905	The Japanese and Korean Exclusion League is created.
1915	The Armenian Genocide occurs.
1917	Literacy tests for immigrants are adopted.
1924	The Immigration Act of 1924, also known as the Johnson-Reed Act, is developed. This legislative piece includes the National Origins Act and the Asian Exclusion Act.
1934	The Philippine Independence Act, also known as the Tyding McDuffie Act, is developed that provided self government and eventual independence to Filipinos. It also restricted Filipino immigration.
1939–1945	World War II and the Holocaust occur.
1942	Internment of Japanese Americans begins.
1942–1964	Bracero Program is in effect.

1943	The Magnuson Act, which repeals the Chinese Exclusion Act of 1882, is developed.
1945–1946	The Cold War begins.
1946	The War Bride Act is developed.
1948	The Displaced Persons Act is developed.
1952	The Immigration and Nationality Act is developed.
1953	The Refugee Relief Act is developed.
1954	"Operation Wetback" leads to the deportation of more than 1 million Mexican migrants and Mexican Americans, according to U.S. officials.
1957–1986	Dictatorial rule of Haiti is imposed by the Duvaliers.
1959	The Cuban Revolution begins.
1959–1975	The Vietnam War.
1962	The Migration and Refugee Assistance Act is developed.
1964	The Civil Rights Act is developed.
1965	The Immigration and Nationality Act of 1965, also known as the Hart Cellar Act, is developed.
1966	The Cuban Refugee Act is developed that allows more than 400,000 Cubans to come to the United States.
1968	The Bilingual Education Act is developed.
1975	The Communist Pathet Lao assumes power in Lao.
1975–1979	The Khmer Rouge Rule in Cambodia.
1975	The Indochina Migration and Assistance Act is developed.
1979	The Iranian Revolution begins.
	Sandinistas assume power in Nicaragua.
	Soviets invade Afghanistan
1980	The Refugee Act is developed.
	The Mariel boatlift from Cuba brings more than 100,000 Cuban refugees to the United States.
1983	Civil War in Sudan spurs a refugee crisis in the southern part of the country.

1986	The Immigration Reform and Control Act of 1986 (IRCA) is developed.
	Civil unrest begins in Somalia.
1987	Amerasian Homecoming Act.
1988	The Civil Liberties Act is developed. Congress provides $1.5 billion in financial restitution to Japanese-Americans who were in the internment camps during World War II.
1989	Tiananmen demonstrations occur in China.
1989–1990	The Cold War ends and the Berlin Wall and the Soviet Union fall. Communist regimes are overthrown in Poland, Hungary, East Germany, Czechoslovakia, and Romania.
1989–2003	Civil war is fought in Liberia.
1990	The Immigration Act of 1990 is developed.
1991	The Haitian government of democratically elected leader Bertrand Aristide is overthrown.
1991–2002	Civil war is fought in Sierra Leone.
1992–1999	Wars in the former Yugoslavia spur a refugee crisis in the Balkans.
1994	The North American Free Trade Agreement (NAFTA) goes into effect.
	The Taliban assumes power in Afghanistan.
	The Clinton administration restores Aristide back to power in Haiti.
1996	The H.R. 3610 is developed. The bill dealt with the investigation and prosecution of terrorists as well as anti-drug programs and measures to curb illegal immigration.
1997	The Nicaraguan Adjustment and Central American Relief Act (NACARA) is developed.
2000	Immigrant Elian Gonzalez is returned to Cuba from the United States.
2001	On September 11, Al Qaeda terrorists hijack four passenger airplanes and crash them into the World Trade Center, the Pentagon, and a field in Pennsylvania.
	On October 7, in retaliation, the United States strikes against Al-Qaeda and the Taliban in Afghanistan.

	On October 26, the United States passes the Uniting and Strengthening America by Providing Appropriate Tools Required to Intercept and Obstruct Terrorism Act (USA PATRIOT Act).
2002	On January 23, the Department of Homeland Security is developed.
	On November 25, the Homeland Security Act is developed.
2003	The Immigration and Naturalization Service (INS) is dissolved and three different departments are created in its place: U.S. Citizenship & Immigration Services (USCIS), U.S. Customs and Border Protection (CBP), and Immigration and Customs Enforcement (ICE).
	War and Occupation of Iraq.
	Civil war in Darfur creates another refugee crisis in Sudan.
2004	The Minuteman Project is founded.
	Bertrand Aristide is overthrown once again by a rebellion in Haiti.
2005	The Border Protection, Antiterrorism, and Illegal Immigration Control Act of 2005 is developed.
2006	On May 1, "A Day Without an Immigrant" protests occur.
	On May 15, the U.S. government declares "Operation Jump Start" and orders the deployment of thousands of National Guard soldiers to assist the Border Patrol in their efforts to control illegal migrants crossing the Mexican American border.
	On October 26, the Secure Fence Act authorizes the construction of a fence along the Mexican American border.
2009	Members from the Somali immigrant community in Minneapolis raise concerns that teenagers in their family could be terrorist recruits.
2010	A massive earthquake strikes Haiti.

1

COMING TO AMERICA: MIGRATION STORIES

Immigration today impacts every corner of the United States and much of the world. In most societies that are greatly influenced by immigration, there are debates about this phenomenon involving the opportunities that immigration can provide as well as the negative consequences it can have for both the migrants and the receiving societies.

To gain a better understanding of the daily life of the recent wave of immigrants, we have to first understand their motivations to come to the United States. There are a variety of reasons why people leave their homelands. Many are looking for adventure and new opportunities, or they move for personal reasons. Others are in search of a better economic situation, and they desire to improve their quality of life. Again for others, the reasons are political, or they have to do with concerns about personal safety as well as that of their family.

Migrants leave their societies because they flee war, violence, a repressive political regime, or they are in search of more social or religious freedom or cultural stability and security. In numerous instances, however, the motivations to leave one's home cannot be as clearly delineated, and a good number of people immigrate because of a combination of economic and security concerns.

IMMIGRATION IN HISTORICAL AND GLOBAL PERSPECTIVE

Immigration is by no means a new phenomenon. Human migration has been part of world history from its earliest days when the first humans are believed to have moved out of Africa. There were various pre-modern waves of migration, such as the Polynesian migration in the Pacific Ocean or the peopling of the Americas by the forebears of today's Native Americans. The creation of European empires and the colonization of the Americas were accompanied by the forced migration of African slaves during the trans-Atlantic slave trade from the sixteenth to the nineteenth century. By the nineteenth century, indentured servants from Asia were also actively recruited to supply the labor needs of the European empires around the world. Furthermore, colonization and imperialism were accompanied by the voluntary mass migration of Europeans who began to settle all over the world.

Industrialization in the Western world in the second part of the nineteenth century and the twentieth century also spurred immigration. For instance, this phenomenon drove immigration to the United States from the years of the Civil War to the 1920s as well as in post-World War II European countries like Germany.

Throughout world history, political crisis and warfare has spurred migration and created huge waves of refugees, a trend that is likely to continue in the future. For example, this occurred during the partition of India and Pakistan in 1947, when millions of people were on the move after the subcontinent gained independence from Britain. Because of the tremendous violence at the time, many Hindus moved to what would become India, and numerous Muslims moved to the newly created country of Pakistan. Large waves of refugees could also be seen in the aftermath of World War II, during the creation of the state of Israel as well as during the wars in Southeast Asia, Afghanistan, and during many other conflicts in numerous parts of the world.

In recent decades there has been an increase in immigration, and this development has global implications. A scholar of international migration observes:

There are more international migrants today than ever before and their number is certain to increase for the foreseeable future. Almost every country on earth is, and will continue to be affected. Migration is inextricably linked with other important global issues, including development, poverty, and human rights. Migrants are often the most entrepreneurial and dynamic members of society; historically migration has underpinned economic growth and nation-building and enriched cultures. Migration also presents significant challenges. Some migrants are exploited and their human rights abused; integration in destination countries can be difficult; and migration can deprive origin countries of important skills.

The United States is believed to receive about 20 percent of total international migration. This is in a world where about 1 in 35 people is estimated to be an immigrant.[1]

In the last few decades, migration and immigration have become intrinsically linked with a phenomenon known as "globalization."

Globalization is the "buzzword" of our time. It describes political, economic, social, and cultural processes that shape our modern world today. Since the 1990s, globalization has been a widely used concept by the media, politicians, academics, and many others, though there is some debate among scholars about how recent this phenomenon really is. Globalization creates or reinforces interconnectedness between different parts of the world and is believed to spur social change.

The processes of globalization that have expanded since World War II have also spurred immigration. To a certain extent the increase is an outgrowth of a gradually more interconnected world. It is partly stimulated because travel has become easier. Furthermore, people have a desire to immigrate because information travels and is distributed at a much faster rate today than in earlier times. It is not unusual to go to many places around the world and have an educated conversation not only about American politics and the economy but also about aspects of American culture and quality of life. To people who live in comparatively poorer conditions, the dream of being able to immigrate to the West to improve one's quality of life can be appealing.

MIGRANTS: REFUGEES AND IMMIGRANTS

This section looks at the migration histories of various immigrant and refugee communities. It examines the motivating factors that led people to come to the United States and explores some of the phenomena and connections that result from immigration. Because the histories of refugee communities are often unique and stem from very complex historical situations, several of them are discussed individually. However, it is also important to underscore that not everybody who belongs to a certain migrant community that has historically been granted political asylum in the United States came to the country as a refugee. For example, the city of Lowell in Massachusetts has a large Cambodian population. The first wave of Cambodians, who came to the city in the 1980s, came as refugees. In recent years, however, their ranks were joined by people of Cambodian origin who have come to the United States more recently and who are not considered refugees. Furthermore, the lines between immigrants and refugees can be blurred at times. Sometimes people escape danger or a politically challenging or threatening situation by obtaining immigration papers through family members or by applying for them at an American embassy rather than applying for political asylum.

Retirement and environmental issues are two other factors that can entice people to migrate. Retirement migrants generally are people at the end of their work life, who decide to leave for areas that provide them with a lower cost living or a nicer climate, or they move to an area to which they have an emotional attachment. In the last decade or so, for example, there has been a growing number of Americans who retire in Mexico.

Natural disasters that cause long-term destruction also can lead to migration. Whether it is desertification of once arable land, natural disasters such as hurricanes, floods, storms, tsunamis, or earthquakes, the destruction left behind by these catastrophes can spur people to move away in an effort to try their luck somewhere else. While environmental migration is often internal, meaning it stays within the original nation-state, it can also be international.

Gradual environmental degradation can also aid in increasing international migration. In the Sahel Zone, for example, the region south of the Sahara desert on the African continent, the expansion of the desert spurred by climate change is increasingly undermining the ability of many of the residents to make a living as herders or farmers, forcing them to move to new locations either in or outside of Africa. While these developments are not the only factors that encourage international migration, it has certainly been one of several reasons why people in this region try to find a way to get to Europe, the United States, or North Africa in search of a better life.[2]

The definitions of migrant, immigrant, and refugee are broad and fluid. The United Nations defines a migrant—a category that includes immigrants and refugees—as a person who lives outside of his or her country of citizenship for at least a year. At times, migrants decide to return to their home country after spending years and even decades away. Frequently, however, immigrants and refugees become citizens of their adopted countries.

Facing Challenges

Immigrants and refugees face many challenges when they relocate to the United States. Something as simple as weather and climate can require difficult adjustments. Someone coming from a tropical or sub-tropical country might experience snow and cold temperatures of the upper Midwest or the Northeast for the first time in their life. Dealing with a cold, cutting wind, walking on ice and snow, figuring how to dress appropriately for such conditions and, in the instances of poorer refugees and immigrants, finding the means to pay for such clothing, are trials and lessons that many newcomers have had to face. Differences in foodstuff and customary table manners can be another issue. Someone who is accustomed to eating a diet based on rice and eating with his or her hands or chopsticks will need to, at least on occasion, adjust to eating with fork and knife and will have to get used to eating American and Western-style foods when they are not able to cook for themselves or if ethnic restaurants are not available.

There are other challenges too. For example, many cultures have different rules or expectations about "appropriate behavior," such as how to stand in line or how to greet people. The "right" behavior in one place is not necessarily suitable in a different country. Figuring out how public transport works, appropriate driving regulations, and how to cross the street sometimes have to be learned as well because migrants sometimes have other sets of rules in their countries of origin. They may also need to adapt to unfamiliar kitchen appliances, bathrooms, showers, and furniture. While such challenges can be uncomfortable or embarrassing experiences, they are minor obstacles that immigrants and refugees can quickly learn to overcome.

However, newcomers to the United States can face more severe trials and ordeals. Language is a major issue for those immigrants for whom English is not their first language. It is hard to learn a foreign language even under ideal circumstances. It gets progressively harder as one gets older. A significant number of immigrants have also had little formal education in their previous life, and many often work two or three jobs, raise families, run households, and are members of religious institutions and cultural organizations where English is not the first language of communication. Thus, some have only a rudimentary knowledge of English, and in other cases they have none at all.

Poor language skills limit the job opportunities of foreign-born workers and make it harder for them to access services. Illiteracy further undermines the career possibilities of some immigrants. Nonetheless, it is important to remember that this situation is in no way dissimilar from that of earlier generations of newcomers. Many earlier immigrants, then mostly of European background, did not learn English either. They often ended up living in Italian, Greek, Polish, Jewish, or German neighborhoods and enclaves, where many spoke in their native tongue exclusively. It was only the subsequent generations that learned English. Even for those immigrants who might have had some education in English in their countries of origin, life is not without its challenges. The American accent and local idiomatic expressions are likely to be different from the English that they were taught at school, and this unfamiliarity requires some adjustment.

Speaking with an accent is also an issue for many immigrants. Some who have an excellent working knowledge of English and have marketable skills believe that they were likely turned down for employment because of the way they talk. This can even be the case for those newcomers for whom English is their first language, as is the case of many immigrants from India or from several countries on the African continent.

IMMIGRANTS

An immigrant is a person who moves from one nation-state to another. There he or she, often alongside family, settles down and establishes residence, which means he or she lives in the country for more than one year. Furthermore, immigrants, as they are defined in this section, are in compliance with the immigration laws of their adopted country.

Why Do People Migrate?

There is a strong desire by many people in what is often referred to as developing countries to move to more affluent parts of the world, such as the United States, western Europe, Canada, Australia, and New Zealand. Even in the most remote corners of the world, Western—and in particular American—media, popular culture, and products have an impact. Hollywood movies are not only blockbusters in the United States, but they reach a global audience. American and Western pop, rock, and hip hop music have become global products and cultural phenomena. TV shows and series from the United States and the Western world are also broadcast to poorer nations.

The stories and images that American and Western mass consumer culture create frequently depict an easy, affluent, and appealing life. For people who work as subsistence farmers or poor urban dwellers, scraping by on little or almost no money, these images spur powerful dreams of a better life. Furthermore, media images of affluence appeal to members of the middle class in developing countries, who are often frustrated with government corruption and inefficiencies. The dream to achieve a better life in a Western country like the United States and all the "opportunities" this provides is seen as a ticket out. Immigrants who live in the United States often comment on the fact that these issues attracted them to move to the country.

Education

Since the 1950s and 1960s, the United States's sophisticated system of higher education has attracted many foreigners to come to America to pursue their studies. Foreign-born students play an important role in higher education. In 2006, 35 percent of all Ph.D. degrees were awarded to foreign-born researchers. In engineering and the sciences over two-thirds of doctorate degrees were earned by people who were not American citizens. This is a significant contribution to the country's system of higher learning. It aids America to stay intellectually competitive, but it also enriches the United States financially. Many foreign-born students remain in the country and become citizens, where they serve as innovative and productive members of the economy.[3]

Immigrants with Desirable Skills and the Issue of Brain Drain

Immigrant visas are also given to foreigners with special skills that are desired in the United States. These can range from medical professionals to computer software engineers, who are of use to the American economy. As the country faces personnel shortages in the medical or other fields of science, recruiting skilled and educated foreigners can alleviate such problems. Coming to the United States also provides advantages to the migrants. The move often means higher salaries and an improvement in their quality of life.

Furthermore, globalization has spurred the movement of highly skilled labor. Multinational corporations in certain economic sectors move a growing number of their employees internationally. Numerous nation-states accommodate the needs of those businesses by granting selective visas to workers, which provide a high degree of mobility to people who have become known as inter-corporate transferees.

There can also be a negative side to the hiring of foreign-born and foreign-educated specialists, however, and the issue has caused some controversy. Such moves are believed by some to depress the wages of American doctors, scientists, nurses, and other members of the middle class. In addition, there is a fear that the United States could become dependent on the outside world to provide certain necessary skills for its economy to stay competitive, such as in the field of science, technology, and medicine. Others argue that fixing problems by bringing in educated outsiders is not a solution, but rather leads the country to avoid addressing systemic educational problems and reforms.

At the same time, in many cases nurses, doctors, engineers, and other educated people come from, and have been trained in, countries that have serious shortages of skilled laborers in such areas. This phenomenon is often referred to as the "brain drain." A quote by the protagonist in the novel *Zenzele*, who chastises a character who left his native Zimbabwe to move to the West, provides a glimpse at how many people in the non-Western world feel about the loss of skilled people:

Africa needs the hearts and minds of its sons and daughters to nurture it. You were our pride. . . . When you did not return, a whole village lost its investment. Africa is all that we have. If we do not build it, no one else will. . . . Yes you are just one, but it is the thousands like you, whom our churches and governments pour money into, who ultimately drain our resources. If our brightest minds go and never return, then it is no wonder that we have poor leadership to guide our nations that we have no engineers to run our machinery, no doctors to staff our hospitals, no professors to fill our universities, and no teachers to educate the generations to come. How can we move forward if our future Mandelas are content to spend their days sipping cappuccinos in Covent Garden? If our potential Sembenes are happier shooting French films in Paris or our Achebes-to-be prefer to tell the stories of Americans, is it surprising that we appear to be culturally void? Who is left to us? You are the epitome of the brain drain.[4]

As this passage demonstrates, the often poor home countries invest a lot of their valuable and limited resources to train professionals, only to lose those skilled laborers to a much wealthier nation in the Western world. These losses can be especially painful in such crucial fields as science, engineering, medicine, and business.

However, there is another side to the story that complicates the situation. Many professionals in the non-Western world leave their home countries because they feel that the resources and facilities to advance their careers are missing. They fault local political leadership for failing to provide adequate conditions. They often deal with unreliable power supplies, missing critical equipment, lack of funds, just to mention a few challenges, that impede highly skilled workers from doing their job and from pursuing their careers. Thus, offers to relocate to universities and labs in the Western world can be tempting. "Many of the brightest and best African scientists," the BBC reports, "have already been lured to the West by the promise of better pay and—more importantly—the chance to carry out more effective research."

Better working conditions, alongside better living conditions, entice numerous educated people in the non-Western world to relocate to Western countries. There, many become citizens of the societies that have lured them.[5] One Filipina immigrant who worked as a nurse explained her decision to stay in the United States. "I like it a lot better here, because I have a future here. I don't have a future there. Because over there I would have to call up my uncle or my uncle's friend to ask him to help me to do this or that, such as get a job."[6]

Not all scholars of global migration see the brain drain as having harmful influences on poor countries exclusively. Some suggest that countries can potentially gain from having their highly skilled citizens working abroad. Some argue that "the recent experiences of countries like India and China suggest that short-term brain drain may generate long-term gains," and that "anecdotal evidence suggests that first-generation brain-drain migrants have managed to build technology bridges that span the divide separating developing and developed world." The contacts, resources, capital, and skills obtained by the immigrants abroad can be of benefit to the sending society, especially if the migrants remain in close touch with their home society or decide to return after having spent some time abroad.[7]

IRREGULAR IMMIGRANTS

"Illegal," "undocumented," or as some scholars prefer to call it, "irregular" immigration, is different from regular immigration because these migrants have either crossed borders in violation of their host countries' laws or they have overstayed their visas. The issue of irregular immigration has dominated the media headlines in the Western world for the last three decades. It is important to acknowledge, though, that most immigration experts estimate that the numbers of irregular migrants are much smaller than those of regular migrants. However, as Western countries are restricting the legal movement of migrants, irregular migration is likely to increase.

In fact, migrant smuggling and human trafficking is a multibillion-dollar global industry.

Defining Irregular Immigrants

There is a vibrant and heated debate about the issue of irregular immigration. Some scholars of international migration argue that the only way irregular immigration will stop is if we alleviate poverty in developing countries and thus take away the incentives for people to migrate in search for a better life.[8] Others advocate for tougher border controls to undermine migration, legal as well as illegal, as they see immigration as a threat to the American way of life—economically, politically, and culturally. Some even polemically link immigrants to terrorism, and they believe that the construction of a border fence will undermine "illegal immigration."[9]

In the past, many scholars have argued that irregular immigrants were motivated by economic hardship to migrate. "Illegal immigrants," writes one historian, have "less education and are poorer than their legal counterparts. Many were nearly poverty stricken and the incentive for migration was strong."[10] There is much to this statement. Many immigrants and many of the world's poorest individuals express a desire to migrate due to their dire economic situation.

Other scholars, however, argue that the poverty that pushes people to migrate is relative. They maintain that irregular Mexican immigrants, for example, are attracted to the United States by the comparatively higher wages they can earn there, but that they often do not leave destitute poverty behind. These academics maintain that irregular immigrants, despite frequent popular claims to the contrary, do not abuse the welfare system in the United States, and that many pay taxes. They also wonder about the effectiveness that immigration policies, such as increased border patrols and the building of a border fence, will have on undermining irregular migration. In fact, several scholars believe that many motivated and resourceful migrants search for ways around the controls and find alternative routes to get into the United States.[11]

Irregular immigrants face many challenges. Due to their status, they are prone to be economically and socially exploited. As irregular immigrants are reluctant to contact the police or other authorities when they are mistreated or taken advantage of, they are frequently preyed upon. They generally live in fear of the authorities. One Caribbean immigrant who initially lived in the United States without papers describes these emotions, "When I saw a policeman on the subway, I'd think he could come and arrest me right now. Once I laughed to myself at the thought, and the policeman looked right at me. Being illegal made me feel horrible."[12] These concerns are not unjustified. Beyond the risk of arrest and deportation, irregular immigrants, on occasion, have also fallen victim to police brutality.[13]

The pathways of irregular immigrants into the United States can be quite dangerous. As we will see below, there are frequent reports in the media of people who are paying their efforts to come to the United States with their lives. Tougher border controls in recent years have also made it less likely for illegal immigrants to return to their country of origin to visit family—cutting them off from their loved ones.

While we often hear in the media attention-grabbing headlines about migrants illegally entering the United States through dangerous deserts or by stormy sea, the reality of many border crossings is not as extreme. It is important to remember that many irregular immigrants arrive in the United States "legally," such as on a tourist or a student visa. They then overstay their visas, thereby becoming "illegal" immigrants.

During his failed efforts to advocate for a temporary worker program, a strategy that some advocates hoped would regulate migration to the United States, then President George W. Bush observed sympathetically about irregular immigrants early in 2004:

Their search for a better life is one of the most basic desires of human beings. Many undocumented workers have walked mile after mile, through the heat of the day and the cold of the night. Some have risked their lives in dangerous desert border crossing, or entrusted their lives to the brutal rings of heartless smugglers. Workers who seek only to earn a living end up in the shadows of American life—fearful, often abused and exploited. When they are victimized by crime, they are afraid to call the police, or seek recourse in the legal system. They are cut off from their families far away, fearing if they leave our country to visit relatives back home, they might never be able to return to their jobs.[14]

This quote in many ways summarizes the motivations as well as the challenges that many irregular migrants face in their daily lives.

Dangerous Crossings

Illegally entering the United States is a perilous strategy. The efforts made by migrants to cross into the United States—whether they come by land or sea—can come at a high price. Some pay with their lives. Yet, many who come in search for work, new opportunities, and a better life, are still willing to take this risk.

For decades immigrants have entered or have tried to enter the United States by boat. Many refugees from Cuba, for example, have taken this often dangerous route. One immigrant described his harrowing experience of being caught in a storm during the crossing from Cuba to Florida:

We had no orientation that night. It was raining so hard—the drops fell with such force that they burned my face. There was such a strong wind that we lost control

Cuban refugees arrive on the Florida coast in a makeshift vessel. J. B. Russel/ Sygma/CORBIS.

of the boat.... [T]he water around us was high. Also if you were not awake, you could tip the boat over.... When a lot of water poured into our boat, we tried to bail it out with a boot.[15]

Many Cubans who flee by boat to the United States are fortunate in a sense that when they survive the dangerous crossing, they are generally given legal status in the United States. This means that they can earn a path to citizenship. But many other immigrants do not have this privilege. Haitians are one of those groups. Despite the risks involved during the sea journey, as well as having a questionable legal status, the Haitians come in relatively large numbers. The *South Florida Sun Sentinel* writes that "in the five-year period from 2003 to 2007, the Coast Guard intercepted 10,000 Haitians. Of those, 1,610 were intercepted in 2007, 1,198 in 2006 and 1,950 in 2005. During periods of particular turmoil, 2,013 aspiring immigrants were turned back in 2003 and 3,229 in 2004 according to Coast Guard figures." This peak in numbers coincided with the second overthrow of Bertrand Aristide's government in Haiti, a *coup d'etat* that was accompanied by a fair amount of instability, violence, and tensions in the country.

There have also been concerns about food shortages that have hit Haiti in 2008, and which some believe might spur an increased exodus of migrants in the future. Attempting to reach the United States can be a risky pursuit. Being caught by American authorities is only one challenge that migrants face. There are also reports about migrants that need to be rescued because their boats capsize. At times, immigrants are not so lucky, and they drown. In a particular tragic accident in April 2008, 15 Haitians drowned and a likely 10 more were presumed dead, though their bodies could not be found to verify their fate.[16]

Large numbers of migrants from Central and South America enter the United States by crossing the southern border of the United States illegally. Many pay people to professionally smuggle them or their family across the border. These individuals are called coyotes. One Latino immigrant living in southern California, who wanted to be reunited with her children, explained the process:

I went to see a woman who told me that she knows a man who knows somebody. She said, "Don't worry." I gave her my phone number and the woman who brought them called me and told me it would cost $600, but that in an hour and a half I would have my children.[17]

Other migrants strike out on their own, or in groups, and try to cross the border by themselves without the help of smugglers. Some migrants get arrested by federal authorities during their efforts to cross the border. Others lose their lives trying to get to the United States, dying of heat exhaustion, thirst, or in accidents. Still, it is important to emphasize that while there are certainly risks involved in crossing the border, only an extremely small minority dies during the endeavor. Thus, the risks are not strong enough deterrents for migrants who use this route.

Immigrants who cross the Mexican-American border face a dangerous terrain. Much of the area is a rough and challenging desert landscape. People can run the risk of dying of thirst and heat exhaustion. The crossing into the United States has become part of Mexican corridos and legends. One passage provides a glimpse of the migrant's experience. It tells the story about how some migrants have left their small town in Durango to seek a new life in the United States. They are caught ill prepared in the desert, exhausted to the point of no return by the heat. They are dying as vultures are circling in on them. One cries out, "We couldn't make it," and the dying young men worry about "How I hurt my mother!"[18] As this story depicts, at times migrants lose their lives in their effort to cross into the United States, leaving their loved ones behind. On numerous other occasions, heat-exhausted migrants close to the point of collapsing are picked up by the border patrols or are rescued by passersby.

The Rio Grande River and the other waterways that run along the U.S.-Mexican border pose another potential challenge to migrants. In fact, these border crossings can be even more dangerous than the desert. According to one study, between 1993 and 1996, 851 people died trying to cross the border this way. This was about 72 percent of the total official

Irregular immigrants arrested crossing the border near Tucson, Arizona. George Steinmetz/CORBIS.

number of casualties of 1,185 who died along the frontier that divides America from its southern neighbor. A Mexican immigrant explains the dangers involved in getting across the water:

Crossing the river can be very dangerous, especially if you cross alone. There are fast water currents, and sometimes the water is quite high. If you don't know how to swim, the undercurrents can pull you right down. And in places the bottom of the river is like quicksand that can trap you. The water turns into kind of a funnel that can drag you down. Some friends of mine have died.[19]

Yet water and desert are just some of the natural trials that immigrants have to face on the southern border. There are also human-inflicted tribulations. One danger that migrants face during their border crossings is crime. There are criminal gangs and individuals who rob people of their wallets, purses, watches, jewelry, and backpacks. These criminals are often armed. There are also reports of rape and other violent crime.[20]

    Immigration authorities, often called *la migra* by Spanish-speaking immigrants, pose another challenge to migrants crossing the border. Since the 1960s, migrants have often been arrested when trying to cross the border. One immigrant describes the interactions with the patrolmen:

They arrest you, ask the usual question. If you get rough, they will get rough, too. Otherwise they are fine. It all depends on the person who arrests you. If he has a mean personality, he will treat you rudely, whether you are impolite or not. But most of the time, it is a routine procedure.

The migrants are arrested for a while and then driven back to Mexico. In many instances they return within in a few days.[21]

While Central and South America are a major source of irregular migrants to the United States, newcomers who enter the country without any documentation come from many other parts of the world. People interested in migrating to the United States, and who can afford it, are willing to pay thousands upon thousands of dollars to get to the country from places like Asia or Africa. Sophisticated, professional illegal networks, which specialize in human smuggling, have filled this lucrative illicit market niche.

Migrants are smuggled into the country via boat and airplane, but often also via land routes through either Canada or Mexico. For decades there have been reports about irregular aliens from Asia, Africa, and the Middle East, who fly into airports like Mexico City, travel up north by road, and then cross the border into the United States, very often assisted in this endeavor by professional smugglers. It is believed that many of them pay thousands of dollars for the journey. The money is either paid in cash out of the individuals' or their friends' and family's savings, or the migrants end up in a kind of indentured servitude situation, where the illegal aliens work in slave-like conditions in the country in places like sweat shops, restaurants, or as prostitutes.

Once in the country, the migrants are often completely and utterly beholden to their masters. This is a topic further explored in Chapter 2, but it is important to remember that illegal entry is not always as dramatic as media accounts suggest. Those irregular immigrants with financial resources can arrive in style and comfort by using high-end, people-smuggling organizations. Many others enter on tourist visas, while still others are smuggled in via the trans-Pacific or the trans-Atlantic sea route.

REFUGEES

Since World War II the United States has become the home of a number of refugees from all over the world. In the past, there has been a bias in American immigration policy to provide preference to people who escaped from what were frequently described as "communist" countries. Many refugees in the United States have thus come from places such as the former Soviet Union, China, Southeast Asia, the eastern European states, and Cuba. Despite this ideological bias, the United States has provided sanctuary to refugees from a variety of other conflicts and oppressive regimes around the world. It is also important to note that since arriving in the United States, many refugees have become American citizens. This section examines the history of some of the major refugee groups that have come to the United States. A basic understanding of their stories provides a glimpse of the interests, motivations, and challenges that many of these communities have faced and will face in their daily lives in the United States.

Global Refugees and the Cold War

Many of the refugees who came to the United States, especially until the 1980s, were from communist nations. Between 1945 and 1989, a period that historians call the Cold War, the United States was the leading power of a Western alliance, represented by a military treaty system called the North Atlantic Treaty Organization (NATO). The Western coalition was based on the principles of free market capitalism and democracy. The Eastern bloc, which the Western alliance opposed, consisted of the Soviet Union and several eastern European states, which formed a military coalition called the Warsaw Pact.

This bloc was ideologically unified by the ideals of communism and socialist democracy. Throughout the Cold War, the United States, the Soviet Union, and their allies were engaged in an ideological struggle that reached far beyond the borders and the reaches of the two alliance systems. The situation was further complicated by the fact that both the United States and the Soviet Union had large stockpiles of nuclear weapons that could virtually guarantee the complete annihilation of the other superpower should the two nations come to blows.

The Cold War was a truly global conflict. The term Cold War stems from the fact that the United States and the Soviet Union never directly fought a war against each other. Globally speaking, however, the term is a misnomer, because the Cold War frequently turned hot. In several places in the non-Western world, such as Korea, Southeast Asia, or Afghanistan, the United States and the Soviet Union became engaged in local wars and conflicts, which resulted from both powers' Cold War strategy. These conflicts are often referred to as proxy wars because one superpower funded and supported military resistance against the other while never openly joining the combat. Such a course was pursued because neither side wanted the other to get ahead or gain an advantage that would then harm the other side's national and strategic interests. However, since both the Soviet Union and the United States had nuclear weapons, no side wanted to go as far as to provoke the other into an extremely destructive conflict.

During the Cold War, the United States pursued a policy that was called containment, which aimed to limit the expansion of communism around the world. Providing a home to exiles from communist nations was seen by many American policymakers as a crucial component in their country's struggle to keep communism at bay. Many American officials believed that communism and socialism victimized people, and that the United States had the moral obligation to take in refugees from the states that had embraced this ideology. Matters were further complicated by the fact that from the 1950s to the early 1980s, several pro-American regimes throughout the non-Western world were destabilized, and some even collapsed and turned socialist. The overthrow of American-supported governments spurred waves of refugees to the United States on several occasions.

Despite a clear bias, it would be unfair to characterize the U.S. refugee policy as merely being driven by Cold War considerations, strategies, and concerns. The policy was in part driven by humanitarian concerns. Over the last few decades the United States has provided a home for refugees from civil wars, oppressive regimes, and gender discrimination.

Cuban Americans

Arguably the group of migrants and refugees most intrinsically connected to the U.S. Cold War and anti-communist policies are Cuban Americans. According to census data, their population in the United States was estimated at 1.3 million people in 2000, which represents roughly 4 percent of the total Hispanic population that year. "Despite their relatively modest numbers," writes one expert, "Cuban Americans are one of the most visible immigrant groups."[22]

While there was some Cuban migration to the United States in the nineteenth and in the first half of the twentieth century, a much more significant number of Cuban Americans has arrived since 1959. It was in this year that a right-wing regime under the leadership of General Fulgencio Batista was overthrown by a left-wing movement, with strong communist leanings under the leadership of Fidel Castro.

The post-1959 migration of Cubans to the United States "took place within the shifting contexts of an internal class struggle, a cold war confrontation, a socialist transformation, the entrenchment of an autocratic political order and an austere economic system in the island, a persistent climate of hostile relations with the U.S., and, at least initially, a favorable, even welcoming reception [of Cubans] in this country." These historic factors are largely the reason why the post-1959 Cuban migration to the United States has been largely middle and upper class, and predominantly ethnically European. Several scholars believe that this is likely an explanation for the relative economic success of Cuban Americans in the United States, especially compared with other immigrant groups.[23]

Some outspoken Cuban Americans have been influential political players who pursue a hostile stance toward the communist regime in Cuba. They have been able to lobby various federal administrations to pursue a hard-line stance against the island nation, for example, by imposing an economic embargo on the country. These policies against Cuba have continued even after the global Cold War ended in the early 1990s.

The political strength and relevance of Cuban Americans is further enhanced by the fact that the population is concentrated in southern Florida. Almost 60 percent of Cuban Americans in the United States live in the greater Miami area, where they are the single largest ethnic group. As Florida has played an important role as a swing state in several of the recent presidential elections, the community has become a sought-after voting block that is courted by politicians.

Southeast Asians

Southeast Asia has also been a region from which the United States has received a number of refugees in the last few decades. Their ranks have been joined by immigrants without refugee status. Many of the Southeast Asian refugees and immigrants, from Vietnam, Cambodia, Laos, Burma, and other countries in the region, have now become American citizens, and many of the more recent arrivals will become citizens in the future.

Vietnam

Vietnamese refugees came to the United States as a result of the Vietnam War that lasted from 1945 to 1975. As part of its broader Cold War strategy to contain the spread of communism, the United States was involved in this conflict for much of its duration and became a major participant in the 1960s. When the United States pulled out its troops from southern Vietnam in 1975, many of the Vietnamese who had fought with or supported the United States against the communist northern Vietnamese and their allies in the south were keen to leave the country. They either did not want to live in a communist country or feared repercussions by the new regime. Many of them faced discrimination and prison.

Many Vietnamese refugees fled the country by boat. Interviews with survivors of this journey provide a glimpse of the horror and the fears that they experienced. "It was a very dangerous journey," one survivor explained. We were in "a little wooden boat about 30 feet long and it carried about 70 . . . 73 people exactly."[24] Throughout their trip, the boat people were in constant fear of bad weather and the possibility that their small boats might sink. Potential pirate attacks that would bring theft, rape, and murder were other perils. The survivors of the dangerous crossing ended up in refugee camps outside of Vietnam, and many came to the United States and other Western countries that were willing to take them in. While Vietnamese refugees were settled all over the United States, over time Vietnamese Americans began to concentrate in particular communities, especially in California or in the Texas cities of Houston and Dallas.

Cambodia

The wave of refugees that came to the United States from Cambodia was closely linked to the rise and fall of the Khmer Rouge regime. In fact, before the rule of the Khmer Rouge, a totalitarian communist movement, the presence of people of Cambodian origin in the United States was quite small. In the early 1970s, Cambodia was led by a general named Lol Nol who had assumed power in 1970. The general was supported by U.S. policymakers who desired a friendly regime in the country because of America's involvement in the war in neighboring Vietnam. Throughout the first half of the 1970s, the Lol Nol government was involved in a civil war with the Khmer Rouge. In this conflict the Cambodian government received support from the United States, which came in the form of military hardware as well as through massive aerial bombings by the American military, which targeted Khmer Rouge-controlled areas.

In April 1975, the Khmer Rouge took over the Cambodian capitol of Phnom Penh and established a regime of terror over the entire country. In their effort to build a classless, agrarian society, the Khmer Rouge forcefully evacuated all cities. During these evacuations many elderly and sick either died while leaving the cities or expired because they were left behind. The Khmer Rouge also abolished private property, money, and all financial structures and closed down schools and Buddhist temples. The regime especially targeted Buddhist monks and other religious leaders, politicians, and government officials affiliated with the Lol Nol government. It also targeted ethnic minorities, artists, people that resisted or were perceived as resisting the Khmer Rouge, educated people, intellectuals, and even at times its own supporters suspected of being traitors.

The Khmer Rouge separated families. It forced Cambodians into labor camps where people lived in horrendous conditions, many dying from exhaustion, malnourishment, torture, or targeted killings. By the time the Vietnamese invaded Cambodia to overthrow the brutal regime, Khmer Rouge misrule had killed an estimated 1.5–2 million people in the country. Cambodia's estimated population prior to the Khmer Rouge had only been at around 8 million.

The Khmer Rouge era prompted a mass exodus out of Cambodia. Hundreds of thousands fled the country, and many ended up in refugee camps in Thailand. Harrowing tales were told of people attempting to flee by boat or trying to cross the border, where they had to fear military attacks or could see loved ones blown to shreds as they stepped on land mines. The Khmer Rouge genocide and the refugee experience left a significant mark on the memory and identity of the community.

This legacy of pain and terror caused by the Khmer Rouge in the Cambodian-American community is apparent in immigrant testimonies. This is even the case when the witnesses were not directly impacted by the regime or experienced this regime at an extremely young age.

The trauma of the parents is thus passed to their children. One person relates her family's experience:

My mom when she talks about the killing fields, I think she ... I ... think that she does have post traumatic stress syndrome, because when I listen to her, her story ... [it is] choppy, but all of them can be pretty violent. ... She actually got tortured. What she told me ... they used to ... put a bag around her neck, and then would suffocate her, and then pour water on her and wake her up again, and then do it to her again. So she went through the camps, and then I think she grabbed her sister, and they, they ran. They left the camp.

The mother's sister was killed days after the flight, not to far from the Thai border, where the two women attempted to flee. "[H]er sister died in her arms ... she had to grab the sarong her parents gave her. That's what she used to wrap her sister up and bury her."[25]

The first wave of Cambodian refuges to the United States arrived from 1975 to 1977. This group was generally well educated, spoke French or English, and had escaped without experiencing the Cambodian "killing fields." The second wave of immigration to the United States occurred after Vietnam overthrew the Khmer Rouge. These refugees had experienced the horrors of the regime, tended to be from rural backgrounds, and had less education. Between 1980 and 1985, the United States took in an average of about 20,000 Cambodian refugees per year. The majority of this population had no or little exposure to Western culture and faced a variety of challenges as they began new lives in the United States. This legacy of terror influences the Cambodian-American community to do this day and has a significant impact on their daily lives.

Bhutan

In more recent years, Bhutan has been a major source of refugees to the global community. The government of the small Buddhist kingdom, located between India and China, expelled more than 100,000 members of its ethnic Nepalese minority in the early 1990s. Since that time, the majority of these refugees have lived in camps in Nepal in deprived conditions. Over a decade after being expelled, a number of Western nations like the United States, Australia, Canada, Denmark, the Netherlands, New Zealand, and Norway have now agreed to a program that will resettle the Bhutanese refugees. The United States offered to provide a home to 60,000.

As with several previous groups of refugees, the transition for Bhutanese exiles to life in the United States is not an easy one. "Everything is strange," explains a refugee, describing the difficult transition that the move from a Nepalese refugee camp to her new home in New York City entailed. "We can't understand anyone, and they can't understand us. We walk on the street, and everybody is a giant. It's scary. We go into the subway it's strange, getting into a lift is odd." Of course, life away from the camp in Nepal is an improvement, as the situation there "was very horrible."

The new life in America can provide challenges to refugees. Many tasks that seem obvious to people who have lived in the United States all their life do not seem that simple to a person who has just moved here from the outside world. Issues such as where to buy groceries, learn English, use public transport or utilities, handle an emergency, obtain an education, find work and health care, as well as many other problems are trials in the daily life of refuges and newcomers. "There's naturally a period of transition and adjustment once they arrive in the (United States)," stated a case worker of the International Rescue Committee, an organization involved in providing assistance to the Bhutanese refugees. This is especially the case for children. "Some of these kids have known nothing but refugee camp life, so when they come to the (United States) they're expected to sit in a classroom, [and] follow a routine they may not be used to."

Many refugees proactively deal with these challenges and try to improve their situation. One Bhutanese refugee states, "For the first couple of days we [were] feeling very lonely, very upset. Now [we are] here for 15 days, everything [is] going smoothly. The goal is to earn money, to be a citizen of a country, to earn a house, and to get freedom and rights . . . that is the goal." Thus, the aspirations of most refugees are not very different from those of many Americans in mainstream society.[26]

Refugees from Right-Wing Oppression

While a considerable majority of refugees in the United States during the Cold War were exiles from communism, there were also a few others that entered the country during this period. However, those who sought political asylum from right-wing regimes supported or put in power by the United States found little support from immigration authorities. For example, among the refugees from the right-wing military dictatorship installed in Chile in the early 1970s, comparatively few were taken in by the United States. Furthermore, Haitians, who fled various right-wing regimes and came to the United States in hope for political asylum and protection encountered a government unwilling to permit them the status of political refugees.[27]

Lost Boys of Sudan and Other African Refugees

It is important to point out that many of the newcomers from Africa are not refugees and that the majority who come to the United States are immigrants. There are, however, a number of Africans who come to America because they are escaping civil wars, ethnic or gender violence, discrimination, and persecution.

In recent years, among African refugees, the most attention has been given to the Lost Boys from Sudan. The Lost Boys are orphans who left behind or lost their families during a civil war in the 1980s and 1990s in southern Sudan. The conflict is believed to have killed as many as 2 million southern Sudanese and displaced millions of others. The violence was spurred when oil reserves were found in the south, and the Sudanese government, which is predominantly controlled by people of northern Sudan, desired to control the new source of wealth.

Furthermore, the population of northern Sudan is Muslim, while many of the southern Sudanese adhere to animist or Christian beliefs. In part, the northern encroachment was also motivated by a desire to convert southerners to Islam. Many Sudanese also imagine the regional division in a racial way. They believe that the northerners are ethnically Arab while the southerners are often described as Africans.

During the civil war, the youth who became known as the Lost Boys were able to escape to refugee camps into neighboring northern Kenya. They often fled under the most horrific conditions—walking barefoot for hundreds of miles, often in desperate search of water and food and fearing attacks from enemies and wild animals. The conflict in southern Sudan has in the last decade or so also spilled over into the Darfur region of western Sudan—where now also, just like in southern Sudan, severe ethnic violence is being committed that many observers again describe as genocide.

Like other refugees to the United States, the Lost Boys confront many challenges. Adapting to daily life in the United States and facing economic and social trials that result from being removed from their familiar culture and networks are the main issues they face in their new home. While their story is powerful and tragic, it is important to remember that it is only one of many refugee experiences from the African continent.

Arab and Iranian Americans

Wars, political unrest, repression, and worries about security have also led people from the Middle East and the Islamic World to leave their home countries. Most of them did not come to the United States as refugees, but were motivated to apply for immigrant visas because they were discontent with the situation in their homelands.

These political reasons notwithstanding, it is important to underscore that many Arabs and Iranians have also come to the United States in search of opportunities and a better life. Thus, the lines between political and economic immigration—between immigrant and refugee—are often blurred. Many of the Iranian or Arab Americans were often of middle-class or upper-middle-class background in their native land before they left for the United States. They often have high levels of education, which prepared them well for their lives in America. Here they earn proportionately high incomes and their families generally continue to do well.

The coming of a new wave of immigrants from the Middle East also led to another significant demographic shift. Arab Americans whose families emigrated from the Middle East to the United States before the 1960s often tended to be Christian. Today, and in more recent decades, the immigrants from the Middle East often tend to be Muslim. Thus, in the last few decades the United States has experienced the emergence of Islam as a noteworthy religion that has become part of the American mosaic.

Iraqis

Over the years the United States has also become the home of refugees and immigrants from Iraq. According to U.S. Census Data from 2000, about 90,000 people who were born in Iraq live in the United States. Though it is hard to determine the exact number, many of these newcomers fled, or were enticed to leave their homeland, due to the brutal rule of the dictator Saddam Hussein. His regime especially targeted ethnic minorities as well as political opponents and their families, who could face imprisonment, torture, murder, and mass killings.

More recently, just as during the U.S. military involvement in Southeast Asia in the 1970s, the war in Iraq in 2003 and the resulting U.S. occupation of the country in the following years has created another refugee crisis that has involved at one time or another more than 4 million Iraqis. While there were millions of people within Iraq who were forced to resettle due to ethnic cleansings, over 2 million Iraqis are believed to have fled the country at the height of the violence. The majority of Iraqis, who are able to afford it, are staying in neighboring Jordan and Syria. There they often are in dire economic straits, unable to find work to sustain themselves and their families. Especially hard hit were those Iraqis who collaborated with the Americans. A newspaper reported in 2007:

Ali Saleh, a 37-year-old interpreter who worked for the military for four years, said he was barely able to leave his neighborhood in western Baghdad, never mind travel with his wife and 2-year-old son to Jordan, where border authorities turned away one of his friends. He traveled to Syria last year to apply, but gave up, fearing the Syrian police officials knew about his American ties when they questioned him roughly at the border. In his four years of work, eight colleagues have been killed. He quit this spring, when a woman working as an interpreter from a different camp was kidnapped and killed in his neighborhood. Yet, he said, "The U.S. Embassy in Baghdad is not for us. Nobody can go there."[28]

The United States and the international community, despite promises to help by providing Iraqis with asylum, have not been forthcoming with much assistance. According to *The Economist*, only 2,600 Iraqis were allowed to enter the United States in 2007. Compare this with the much smaller country of Sweden, which granted 19,000 Iraqis formal refugee status in the same year.[29]

Regional experts hope that with the currently improving security situation in Iraq, a growing number of refugees will return to the country, a trend that, as observers note, has started to happen in 2008. Yet, the situation in Iraq remains volatile, and this trend could be reversed should the situation deteriorate again.

TRANSNATIONAL AND DIASPORA LIVES

As processes of globalization make our world more interconnected, these developments are certainly having an impact on the daily lives of immigrants. Due to technology, faster ways of travel, and improved ways of communications, today's newcomer communities have a much easier time maintaining close links with their countries of origin, especially when compared with immigrants from a century ago. Scholars have used two concepts to describe such global connections: diaspora and transnationalism.

One scholar describes "[m]odern diasporas" as "ethnic minority groups of migrant origins residing and acting in host countries but maintaining strong sentimental and material links with their countries of origin."[30] Historically the term is often used to describe the experience of the Jewish community, but it has also been used to illustrate the African or Armenian experience. Similarly, scholars apply the term to describe the migratory processes of Chinese, Indian, and various other communities. The sociologist Robin Cohen provides a useful, expansive definition of the term:

1. Dispersal from an original homeland, often traumatically, to two or more foreign regions;
2. Alternatively, the expansion from a homeland in search of work, in pursuit of trade, or to further colonial ambitions;
3. A collective memory and myth about homeland, including its location, history, and achievements;
4. An idealization of the putative ancestral home and a collective commitment to its maintenance, restoration, safety, and prosperity, even to its creation;
5. The development of a return movement that gains collective approbation;
6. A strong ethnic group consciousness sustained over a long time and based on a sense of distinctiveness, a common history, and the belief in a common fate;
7. A troubled relationship with host societies, suggesting a lack of acceptance at the least or the possibility that another calamity might befall the group;
8. A sense of empathy and solidarity with co-ethnic members in other countries of settlement; and
9. The possibility of a distinctive, creative, enriching life in host countries with a tolerance for pluralism.

These common features indicate strong international connections of diaspora communities.[31]

Transnationalism, an organizing principle that has been popular among numerous scholars in recent years, is also a concept used to describe the links and frequent connections between immigrants in the United States and their home countries. Transnational communities are "[d]ense networks across political borders created by immigrants in their quest for economic advancement and social recognition. Through these networks, an increasing number or people are able to live dual lives." The participants in these networks "are often bilingual, move easily between cultures, frequently maintain homes in two countries, and pursue economic, political and cultural interests that require their presence in both."[32]

Beyond keeping academics busy theorizing, the sociological phenomena described by the terms diaspora and transnationalism have a serious impact on the daily lives of many immigrants. As we will see in later chapters, many foreign-born residents in the United States maintain continuous social, economic, cultural, and political ties with their country of origin or with family and community members that have migrated to other parts of the globe.

LIVING IN AMERICA: MIXED AND ETHNIC NEIGHBORHOODS

Many of the newly arrived immigrants in the United States live in diverse urban areas. Mega cities like New York, Chicago, and Los Angeles are often referred to as immigrant or gateway cities because they have always had large immigrant populations. Starting increasingly in the last few decades, however, there have been some significant demographic changes in the United States largely brought about by immigration.

Today, as mentioned in the introduction, immigrants live in many parts of the country where they historically had little presence. They do not only live in urban areas anymore, but they are also moving to the suburbs in growing numbers. In the last 15 to 20 or so years the American South and the Midwest have seen a gradual but dramatic growth in immigration. Though traditionally not receiving areas for migrants, both regions now have significant Latino enclaves as well as foreign-born residents from Asia, the Middle East, and Africa.

The major influx of immigrants has aided in the creation of diverse and mixed communities in which newcomers reside side by side with established ethnic groups, such as African, Irish, Polish, Jewish, Russian, German, or Italian Americans—many of which have become part of American mainstream society. All over the United States many immigrants shop alongside their neighbors in supermarkets for groceries or in shopping malls for clothing, shoes, and electronics. They also go to the same movie theaters, restaurants, or doctor, dentist, lawyer, and tax offices. They frequent the same public libraries, YMCAs, pools, hospitals, hair and beauty salons, and gyms.

As we will see in more detail in later chapters, immigrants are changing many neighborhoods and communities. It is not unusual today to find mainline churches, which attract their fair share of newcomers, standing alongside, for example, Korean Presbyterian or Latino Pentecostal churches. Today many towns and cities do not only host churches and synagogues. They are also the homes of Hindu and Buddhist centers and temples, Muslim mosques, Sikh gurdwaras, and many other places of worship. Many shops and businesses are also run by immigrants. These shops can cater to mainstream American customers, but often they are also aimed at consumers of a specific immigrant group. Immigrants are also working in chain restaurants and stores, supermarkets, as well as in manufacturing businesses and factories. They are lawyers, doctors, dentists, and tax accountants.

Acknowledging the demographic changes in the United States, corporations and businesses also have begun to cater to the growing clientele of newcomer populations. For example, supermarkets in areas that have high concentrations of immigrants offer a wide variety of international products, foods, vegetables, and fruits in an effort to suit the tastes of their foreign-born customers. Many car dealerships and other businesses have also begun to hire immigrants. Managers argue that these sales representatives, due to their cultural literacy and language skills, are more effective in serving the needs of the new strata of customers. Mainstream video, book, and music stores have also begun to cater to the wider customer base by renting more foreign films or by selling foreign language music, books, and videos.

The strong influx of newcomers of a particular immigrant group in specific areas has also led to the creation of ethnic neighborhoods or enclaves. Scholars use the term ethnic neighborhood or enclave to describe an area that has a particularly high concentration of a specific immigrant group. The lower Highlands in Lowell, Massachusetts, for example, has a large community of Southeast Asians—especially Cambodians. Throughout this neighborhood, one can find many houses and apartments occupied by Cambodians and other Southeast Asians, but also Cambodian jewelry stores, supermarkets, restaurants, liquor stores, beauty salons, as well as video, appliance, and furniture stores, car repair places, and travel agencies. In the last 20 years or so, the existence of shops and businesses has attracted a number of Cambodian immigrants to move to the city.

In the 1980s, Brooklyn's shorefront peninsula took on many features of a Soviet Jewish neighborhood. The area saw the surfacing of many synagogues and temples, delicatessens that sold caviar, bakeries, butcher shops, nightclubs, Georgian and Ukranian restaurants, a bookstore that sold books written in the Cyrillic alphabet in various Slavic languages,

Chinese immigrants at home in Chinatown, New York City. Catherine Karnow/
CORBIS.

and folk art stores that sprang up during that decade. The area was also
known by some as the "little Odessa by the Sea." The famous Chinatown
in cities like New York or San Francisco are surviving enclaves from the
nineteenth century, but they still attract many Chinese immigrants today.
There are many other examples of ethnic enclaves. Los Angeles has
various areas that are predominately settled by Latinos; several Miami
neighborhoods are dominated by Cuban Americans; Dearborn and parts
of Detroit, Michigan, have a strong Muslim community; and Indian
enclaves can be found in Queens, New York, and in Chicago. Here, alongside the regular ethnic stores and businesses described above, you can
also find the occasional ethnic movie theater, club, cultural institutions,
and community centers.

   Immigration is changing the face of the United States. The migration
stories of the newcomers have had an impact not only with regard to
better understanding certain aspects of their daily life. The presence of
immigrants and foreign-born citizens is truly leaving a mark on the entire
nation, as they are significantly altering the American mosaic.

NOTES

   1. Khalid Koser, *International Migration: A Very Short Introduction* (New York:
Oxford University Press, 2007), 1–4.

2. Rayna Bailey, *Immigration and Migration* (New York: Facts on File, 2008), 15.

3. "Professional News," *NEA Higher Education Advocate*, Vol. 25, February 3, 2008.

4. J. Nozipo Maraire, *Zenzele: A Letter for My Daughter* (New York: Delta Book, 1996), 64–65.

5. Hugh Levinson, "Addressing Nigeria's Brain Drain," March 31, 2008. *bbcnews.com*. http://news.bbc.co.uk/go/pr/fr/-/2/hi/science/nature/7322365.stm (accessed June 17, 2008).

6. "Valerie Corpus, a Skilled Filipina American, Reflects on the Advantages and Disadvantages of Life in the United States, 1979," in *Major Problems in American Immigration and Ethnic History*, ed. Jon Gjerde (Boston: Houghton Mifflin, 1998), 460.

7. Jonathon Moses, *International Migration: Globalization's Last Frontier* (London: Zed Books, 2006), 174–175.

8. Moses, 19–21.

9. Chilton Williamson, Jr. ed., *Immigration and the American Future* (Rockford, IL: Chronicle Press and the Rockford Institute, 2007); Mark Krikorian, *The New Case Against Immigration: Both Legal and Illegal* (New York: Sentinel, 2008); Peter Brimelow, *Alien Nation: Common Sense About America's Immigration Disaster* (New York: Random House, 1995).

10. David Reimers, *Still the Golden Door: The Third World Comes to America*, Second Edition (New York: Columbia University Press, 1992), 209.

11. Douglas Massey, Jorge Durand, and Nolan Malone, *Beyond Smoke and Mirrors: Mexican Immigration in an Era of Economic Integration* (New York: Russell Sage Foundation, 2003).

12. "A Caribbean American Observes Life in New York City, 1971–1976," in *Major Problems in American Immigration and Ethnic History*, 453.

13. "Santiago Maldonado, a Mexican American, Details the Lives of Undocumented Immigrants in Texas, 1994," in *Major Problems in American Immigration and Ethnic History*, 454.

14. "President Bush Proposes New Temporary Worker Program: Remarks by the U.S. President on Immigration Policy, The East Room," January 7, 2004, *The White House*. http://www.whitehouse.gov/news/releases/2004/01/20040107-3.html (accessed July 10, 2008).

15. "A Cuban Flees to the United States," in *Major Problems in American Immigration and Ethnic History*, 457.

16. Mike Clary and Joel Marino, "15 Dead, 10 Migrants Still Missing as Bahamas Search Ends," April 22, 2008, *South Florida Sun-Sentinel.com*. http://www.sun-sentinel.com/services/newspaper/printedition/tuesday/nationwold/sfl-flbhaitian deaths0422sbapr22,0,2618355.sto (accessed May 10, 2008).

17. Quoted in Leo Chavez, *Shadowed Lives: Undocumented Immigrants in American Society* (San Diego: Harcourt Brace Jovanovich, 1992), 59.

18. Quoted in John Annerion, *Dead in Their Tracks: Crossing America's Desert Borderlands* (New York: Basic Books, 2003), 77.

19. See oral history of Jose and Rosa Maria Urbina, "El Paso Del Norte," in *The New Americans and Oral History: Immigrants and Refugees in the U.S. Today*, ed. Al Santoli (New York: Viking, 2008), 269–270.

20. Jose and Rosa Maria Urbina, "El Paso Del Norte," in *The New Americans*, 269–270.

21. Jose and Rosa Maria Urbina, "El Paso Del Norte," in *The New Americans*, 269–270.

22. Lisandro Perez, "Cuba," in *The New Americans: A Guide to Immigration Since 1965*, ed. Mary Waters and Reed Ueada (Cambridge, MA: Harvard University Press, 2007), 386.

23. Perez, 386–398.

24. Tony Mai interviewed by Christoph Strobel, April 24, 2008, Ethnographic Study of Lowell, MA.

25. Sambath Bo interviewed by Christoph Strobel, April 15, 2008, Ethnographic Study of Lowell, MA.

26. "From Bhutan to the Bronx," April 29, 2008. *BBC News.com*. http://news.bbc.co.uk/go/pr/fr/-/2/hi/south_asia/7372916.stm (accessed May 2, 2008).

27. Reimers, 187–193.

28. "Few Iraqis Reach Safe U.S. Havens Despite Program," *New York Times*, August 29, 2007.

29. "Refugees from Iraq," *The Economist*, February 23, 2008, 78–79.

30. Gabriel Scheffer, "Introduction," in *Modern Diasporas in International Politics*, ed. Scheffer (Houndsmill, England: Palgrave Macmillan, 1986), 3.

31. Robin Cohen, *Global Diasporas: An Introduction* (University of Washington Press, 1997), 26.

32. Alejandro Portes, "Immigration Theory for a New Century: Some Problems and Opportunities," *International Migration Review* 31 (Winter 1997), 812.

2

MAKING A LIVING: ECONOMICS

Immigrants play a central role in the U.S. economy. This is a situation not unique to America. In fact, as a growing number of historians, sociologists, and political scientists in the last three decades have pointed out, migration is a global phenomenon that has far-reaching economic implications.

Many of the historical and sociological trends and tendencies that can be observed in America can similarly be witnessed in other societies around the world. While immigration does not play itself out in the same way in different places—acknowledging the fact that every society is indeed different—there are still many similarities in the trends, patterns, and processes that receiving societies and immigrants undergo. Such arguments contradict the claims by previous generations of scholars who argued for "American exceptionalism" with regard to immigration.[1]

It is important to underscore that in the past as well as in the present, immigration had and has a significant global economic impact. A scholar of the current system of international migration observes:

It has been estimated by the World Bank that migrant labour around the world earns U.S. $20 trillion—the vast majority of which is invested in the countries where they work. Another study indicates that about 15 million foreign-born workers in the U.S.A. add over U.S. $10 billion to the U.S. economy. Migrant labour, it is argued, has therefore contributed significantly to economic growth. Throughout much of the world migrants are not only employed in jobs that nationals are reluctant to do, but are also engaged in high-value activities that local people lack the skills to do.[2]

Looking at these numbers, it is likely that migration and immigration will continue to have a significant economic impact—in the United States as well as around the world.

The contributions of immigrants to the economy—whether on a local, national, or international level—is only one part of the story. The personal lives of immigrants are also significantly shaped by economics. In fact, economic factors and circumstances play an important role in the daily life of the newcomers. Like most Americans, immigrants spend a significant amount of time at work. Their professions often influence their social standing in society and can be a source of personal fulfillment or stress.

The issue of immigrants in the economy raises several questions. Where do they work? What is the nature of their jobs? What sectors of the economy are they employed in? What professions do they have? Are they self-employed? Do they work minimum-wage jobs? Were there economic conditions that pushed migrants to move, and if so, what were they? Do economic circumstances shape immigrant settlement patterns? Do ethnic communities and families collaborate, and if so, how, and to what means? These are just a few questions that are grappled with by historians, sociologists, anthropologists, economists, and political scientists interested in learning more about immigrant communities. Furthermore, to scholars interested in the recent history of immigrants, they provide a glimpse at the tremendous economic diversity and complexity among their lives in the United States.

Hence, immigration, economics, and daily life are profoundly interconnected. In sum, immigrants play an important role in the American economy, while economics plays a vital part in the daily life of immigrants.

ROLE OF IMMIGRANTS IN THE ECONOMY

There has been a heated debate about the impact that immigrants have on the U.S. economy. Much of the public discussion either condemns immigration as harmful or commends it as beneficial to American society. Either position provides too simplistic an understanding of the economic impact of immigration.

There are many opponents to the current migration system in the United States—irregular and, in many cases, regular. These critics see immigration as a threat to American society. They argue that irregular immigration is especially harmful to the economy. They believe that too many illegal immigrants lack adequate education, which leads to lower wages, fewer taxes, and the wider use of social services. The high influx of immigrants also reduces the pay of low-skilled American-born workers because the competition weakens their ability to demand higher wages. Furthermore, one critic argues that irregular immigration undermines the economic competitiveness of the United States. "[B]y keeping wages lower, illegal immigration takes away much of the incentive to invest in labor-saving technologies that make workers more productive, thus slowing the innovation that is needed for continued economic vitality."[3]

Other experts disagree. They see the impact of irregular immigration on the economy as generally positive. They argue that immigrants contribute to the economy as taxpayers, workers, and consumers. Irregular immigrants also pay for Social Security and Medicare, even though they are not eligible for these programs. They contribute to economic output, and they are believed to generate more tax revenue than they use in services. Immigrants are the backbone of the labor force, especially in industries such as agriculture, construction, meat processing, grounds keeping, and textile production.[4]

Both the anti- and pro-immigration advocates provide a limited perspective of the economic impact of immigration on the American economy. Immigration comes with costs associated to it, but also with benefits. The debate tends to focus often on irregular immigration, which selectively cuts out much of the immigrant population living in the United States. Furthermore, while irregular migrants violate the laws of the United States by working in the country "illegally," they also fulfill important functions in society.

Most mainstream Americans do not want to experience the conditions under which many immigrant workers toil. They do not want to undergo, for example, the harsh conditions that the daily life of migrant labor entails. This lifestyle requires workers to move every few weeks, live in dormitories without privacy or in housing such as decrepit trailers or in even poorer conditions, where they work back-breaking jobs on farms, potentially exposed to dangerous chemicals, and often for little pay. Similarly, documented and irregular immigrants remain a source for labor in such sectors as construction, meat-processing, landscaping, hospitality, maintenance work, and the garment industry.

These jobs are appealing to migrants in search of better wages and work, but many native-born Americans consider these jobs undesirable. At the same time, while many in the United States complain about the presence of irregular immigrants, American consumers want to buy cheap products. Many, however, close their eyes to the reality that in the effort to maximize profits, to keep prices low, and to stay competitive, many employees resort to cheap labor, and that potentially many of the workers they hire can be in the country "illegally."

The debate about "illegal" migrants has been significant for various reasons. For one, it is about numbers. In 2008, migrants without legal status in the United States were estimated at 12 million to 14 million people. It is important to remember though that this group is a minority among foreign-born residents in the country. Still, irregular immigration is given disproportionate attention, and many of the opinions and perceived notions on this issue are shaping the views of many in the American mainstream about immigration in general. Much of this understanding is too simplistic and ill-informed and leaves too little room for understanding the complex picture of the role that immigrants play in the economy.

Immigrants and immigration has direct and indirect effects, both positive and negative, on the economy. They influence labor markets, fiscal costs as well as revenues, and profit margins. The specific economic impact of immigration depends on a wide variety of factors. One such aspect is the background of immigrants, especially their level of skill and education, but it also depends on issues, such as federal, state, or local public policies, laws, societal factors, and programs. Such dynamics influence the diverse, complex, and multifaceted economic involvements, contributions, and costs of immigration.

The daily life of immigrants and the role that newcomers play in society have been significantly shaped by developments that have transformed the U.S. economy since the 1960s. America has undergone some dramatic changes. Grasping this transformation is not only crucial to understanding the complex and diverse role that immigrants play in the American economy, but it also provides a glimpse at the varied daily life experiences of newcomers to the United States, which are often, at least in part, shaped by immigrants' social and economic backgrounds. In the last three decades in America, jobs in manufacturing and agriculture have declined, while employment in the service sector has increased. The growth of jobs in this area was accompanied by two opposite trends. On the one hand, it has led to an increase in employment for people with advanced degrees— such as engineers, computer specialists, educators, and doctors. Some of these positions have been filled by highly skilled immigrants. On the other hand, and at the same time, the growth in the service sector has also brought a dramatic increase in low-skill employment. This condition can be seen especially in the health care, restaurant, and child care industry, but also in building maintenance, cleaning, and landscaping services, as well as in the meatpacking industry. These jobs pay low wages and require little skill, knowledge of English, or education. Many of these positions have been filled by immigrants.

Since the 1960s there have been three additional major transformations in the American economy. First, the region of the United States often referred to as the Sunbelt, which comprises the southern and southwestern states, has seen spectacular growth in economic activity. The increase in economic output and jobs has led to more immigration in that area.

The second change is the decline of labor unions in the United States, which has undermined the position of workers—whether they are foreign or native born. The weakening of unions could be seen in industries such as meatpacking, maintenance work, as well as in other areas of employment. Today the non-unionized, low-wage, and often dangerous and physically demanding work is not appealing to many native-born Americans—at least not at the wages that employers offer. To immigrants with fewer opportunities in their countries of origin, however, these jobs can be attractive. Yet, this appeal should not be overestimated. There is a high turnover rate for employees in these industries, which seems to suggest that workers leave these positions as soon as they find better work opportunities.[5]

The larger economic transformations in the United States have in turn aided in a third development—a dramatically growing income disparity among low-skill and high-skill employees. Over the last few decades, the wages of individuals with a high school degree have fallen, while those with advanced degrees have increased. The implications for the American economy are significant, as these developments are reinforcing and augmenting processes of inequality that have serious social implications.

Immigrants continue to play a pivotal role in the economic transformation of the United States—both at the high- and low-skill level of the job sector. About 50 percent of jobs generated by the economy between 1990 and the mid-2000s have been filled by foreign-born workers. In 2004, immigrants comprised an estimated 12 percent of the population, but they represented 15 percent of all workers and 20 percent of all low-wage workers.[6]

Many social scientists see migrants as "providing a reserve labor supply."[7] In other words, economies benefit from migrants because they can draw on them at a time when they need employees and might not have enough workers at home. However, the picture is not wholeheartedly positive. Immigration, the drawing from a foreign labor reserve, does not benefit everyone. Several economists argue that it can have a negative impact on native workers with low skills. In some cases employers can potentially use migrants to get their employees to agree to lower wages, or they can replace them altogether with immigrant labor willing to work for less. By hiring immigrant employees, employers can increase their profit margins or lower the prices for the goods they are selling, which can be beneficial to stockholders of companies and to consumers. At the same time, however, there is some debate about how much immigrants really drive down wages. Several scholars argue that foreign competition, the ability of other countries to produce certain types of goods at a significantly cheaper cost than the United States, is really the main driving force behind the decline in the salaries of low-skill workers.

Furthermore, by merely describing people willing to migrate as a "labor reserve" the agency of immigrants is neglected. Social science models and theories might provide a window to understanding immigrants' decisions and motivations, but immigrants are as much motivated by factors that influence their daily life. While economic recessions can certainly slow down the flow of immigrants to a significant level, they are not likely to stop immigration altogether. A certain number of people is likely to continue to come to the United States and other Western countries unless dramatic legal and security barriers that impede the movement of people would be implemented. Even then, irregular and regular migration would likely continue.

There are a variety of explanations for this. For one, the migrant might simply be unaware of the changing economic reality in the country he or she is intending to move to, or he or she might rely on outdated reports. Second, it is often the case that the economic situation in the sending society is worse than in the country of destination. A strong desire to support one's family or improve a loved one's life becomes a strong driving force. Third, it is also important to underscore that migrants have reasons other than economics to move to a new destination. The desire to emigrate might be spurred by political, safety, social, family, or religious reasons, as well as for romantic interests or simply by a sense of adventure.

There is a frequent claim that immigrants take advantage or even abuse the welfare state in the United States. Hence, they are seen by many as a strain on the American economy and social system. While a significant number of low-skill laborers are foreign born, it is important to point out that many of the public assistance programs are not available to all immigrants, but only to refugees who were allowed into the United States due to persecution or endangerment in their home countries. To ease their adjustment to a new life in America, government and non-governmental organizations provide some modest assistance programs. While assistance certainly helps, its general impact and benefits should not be exaggerated, as these types of programs provide minimal contributions. Social programs also vary widely throughout the United States. Furthermore, in many cases immigrants do not utilize the welfare programs that are made available to them because they are too proud to accept help, are too fearful, or they simply do not know that such services are available to them.

Despite frequent concerns about the harmful fiscal effects and costs of immigration to American society, evidence seems to suggest that immigrants also contribute to America's fiscal stability. Certainly immigration creates fiscal costs as newcomers utilize public resources such as schools, hospitals, and a variety of other social programs and services. However, immigrants also pay taxes that pay for these services and they contribute to Social Security and Medicare. Many immigrants come to the United States when they are at a young age and become long-term contributors to these programs that finance the retirement of elderly native-born Americans. Examining the economic data, the National Research Council determined that "[i]mmigrants are a net taxpayer benefit to native-born households. Yet, this net benefit takes place exclusively at the federal level, and not at the state level." So states with higher ratios of immigrants have to bear a higher fiscal burden.[8]

WORKERS

Immigrants play an important role in the U.S. economy as workers. They can be found laboring in all sectors. Regular and irregular immigrants are employed in the service industry, factories, agriculture, meatprocessing, domestic labor, construction, and in high technology. These are just a few areas in which they are employed.

Factory Workers

Even though there has been a decline in manufacturing in the United States in the last few decades, factory jobs are still part of the daily working life of a significant number of immigrants. The experiences of immigrant factory workers are diverse and complex. They work in industrial production facilities that make a wide variety of products and that vary in size. Places of employment can range from the small manufacture that pays a handful of workers to large industrial production facilities that employ thousands of laborers.

Newcomers labor on all shifts and at all hours: first shift (morning to early afternoon), second shift (afternoon to night), and if their work requires it, also the graveyard shift (night). They can be seen working on assembly lines, operating and fixing industrial machinery, and working foundries and various other production processes. While they are often low-skill workers, they can occasionally be highly skilled laborers who have been brought to the United States by their employers for their high-level proficiencies. Nevertheless, for the most part, like American-born workers, immigrants who work in manufacturing are vulnerable to plant closings and job cuts due to downsizings, mechanization, and outsourcing.

Service Industry

While immigrant laborers work at all levels of the service industry, they are disproportionately represented in entry-level service jobs. Immigrants can be seen operating cash registers in retail stores, stacking shelves in stores, and unloading and uploading trucks that deliver groceries and other goods. They work in barbershops and hair salons washing and cutting their clients' hair. They staff hotel lobbies and clean rooms. They prepare and serve food in restaurants, hotels, and work in the fast-food industry. They bus tables and wash dishes.

Many immigrants also travail in entry-level health care jobs, where they are employed in nursery homes and hospitals. Furthermore, they work in landscape businesses, take care of people's lawns and gardens, and labor in nurseries bringing up plants, bushes, and trees. They work as janitors and custodians, cleaning and maintaining buildings all over the United States.

Meat Cutters

The meatcutting industry is another sector in the American economy that has seen an increase in the use of immigrant labor. This growth has

A Sikh and a Vietnamese immigrant working in the kitchen of an Indian restaurant.
David H. Wells/CORBIS.

coincided with a decline in wages and benefits for meat cutters, despite
the fact that it is a dangerous and challenging profession. Many modern
slaughterhouses are factories where hundreds, and more often thousands,
of heads of animals are killed and processed in a day. Animals like cattle
and swine are marched into the factories, killed, and then often hung up
on conveyor belts where the animals are moved along the plant, to be
dehided or skinned, and then cut and processed.

Unlike in chicken plants, where much of the killing, plucking, gutting,
beheading, and cutting are mechanized tasks performed by machines
and robots, the processing of beef and pork still relies on human labor.
This work is predominantly performed by immigrant workers. Most meat
cutters are of Latino backgrounds and both men and women work in this
industry.

Meat cutters wear protective gear of hard hats and chain mail apron
and gloves, which cover their hands and wrists as well as their upper
bodies. Despite these protective measures, injuries occur frequently.
In his book, *Fast Food Nation: The Dark Side of the All American Meal*, Eric
Schlosser notes:

The injury rate in a slaughterhouse is about three times higher than the rate in a
typical American factory. Every year more than one-quarter of the meatpacking
workers in this country—roughly forty thousand men and women—suffer an

injury or a work related illness that requires medical attention beyond first aid. There is strong evidence that these numbers, compiled by the Bureau of Labor Statistics, understate the number of meatpacking injuries that occur. Thousand of additional injuries and illnesses most likely go unrecorded.[9]

Meatpackers, who work with dangerously sharp knives and other cutting tools, frequently suffer from lacerations inflicted either by themselves or by a coworker operating close by. Furthermore, because the labor is so physically demanding, they frequently suffer from shoulder and back problems, as well as carpal tunnel and "trigger finger" syndrome (the name for a condition in which a finger becomes permanently crippled in a curled position). The risks of injuries in meatpacking plants grow especially when the assembly lines are sped up to increase the rate of production.[10]

The filthiest job in the meatpacking industry is performed by the slaughterhouse sanitation crews. The tasks are generally outsourced to "independent contractors" not officially affiliated with the meatpacking plants. These employers often hire irregular immigrants to perform the dangerous jobs because they are cheaper, but also because they are less likely to be resistant to poor working conditions and scared to get the authorities involved for fear of deportation. The crews clean the factories and machines, conveyor belts, and floors during the night, utilizing high-pressure hoses that spray extremely hot chemical-laden water. After a shift the stench of blood, animal remains, and chemicals is so potent, one worker explains, "that it won't wash off; no matter how much soap you use after a shift, the smell comes home with you, seeps from your pores."[11]

Apart from being the filthiest, the cleaning crews are also believed to have the most dangerous job in the meat plant. While official statistics about labor accidents among the sanitation workers are not being kept, anecdotal evidence from newspapers and reports provides a glimpse of the danger of the working life of these laborers. There are reports of workers being injured or killed by moving conveyor belts during cleaning operations, a worker who was beheaded while cleaning a de-hiding machine, as well as workers who were killed because they fell off machinery that they were in the process of cleaning with high-pressure hoses. In those instances the workers either lost their balance due to the high water pressure or because they slipped on a mixture of hot water, chemicals, animal intestines, and blood, and fell to a concrete floor from some distance above. There are also frequent reports of workers losing fingers or an arm while cleaning machinery in meatpacking plants.[12]

Agricultural Labor

While overall the number of people working in the agricultural sector has declined in the last few decades, it is still an area that employs a large percentage of immigrant labor—regular and irregular. Farm workers pick oranges, lemons, limes, and many other fruits. They harvest different varieties of vegetables grown in the United States. In addition, immigrant laborers work for the agribusiness sector meat production, where they work for businesses that raise chicken, beef, turkey, and pork, often on an industrial scale.

Agricultural work is frequently not stable. Laborers are often employed by the needs of their employers, which depend upon the commodity being produced and the time of the year. This means that on certain days workers are employed for upwards to 18 hours. If employers have no use for workers, however, they cut back on workers or eliminate jobs. Thus, workers will not get hired, and they will not get paid. Furthermore, laborers salaries are generally based on productivity. For instance, a worker is compensated a certain amount of money for each bucket, or certain predetermined weight of a product that they fill or collect and return to the employer.

The working conditions for farm laborers are often difficult. Migrant laborers who harvest lemons and limes can face severe cuts because the plants have thorns on the branches. Picking oranges is also a challenging job. It requires a lot of strength to move a 30-foot ladder from tree to tree. In addition, the pickers carry big bags around their necks, where they store the oranges they harvest. A bag weighs in at over 90 pounds when it is full, making it extremely hard for the pickers to keep their balance on top of the ladder. In addition, they must be careful to keep the ladder from tipping or falling over when they pick fruits from the trees.

Immigrant farm laborers working in the fields of North Carolina. Andrew Lichtenstein/CORBIS.

Injuries and accidents can be detrimental as the workers and their families often have no insurance or access to worker's compensation. Whether they are picking fruits or harvesting vegetables, laborers are exposed to the elements in their work. This can mean working in burning sunshine in 110° hot weather or in a cold, uncomfortable rainstorm, which drenches a person's clothing through to the skin. In general, the pay for immigrant labor in these types of jobs is very low.

There are further challenges for farm laborers, including reports of incidents of sexual harassment, especially of women workers on the job. Furthermore, housing and food costs, often provided by agricultural businesses, are inflated. Many migrant workers do not have access to a car and are therefore forced to pay the high company prices at the local store. This often eats up an entire family's salaries, just as it helps employers to benefit financially, and it can also aid in keeping the workers in a state of dependency. By providing their employees with credit to buy food, for example, employers increase their leverage over their employers as the workers will have to repay their financial commitments in the future.

The social and economic conditions of agricultural laborers can often be challenging. The children of migrant workers frequently do not receive an adequate education. The frequent moving that is often part of the life routine of their parents creates an unstable educational situation for their children that is not conducive to learning. Furthermore, the parents often need the labor of their children out in the fields for their families to financially survive, which means that teenagers are often pulled out of school. Frequently, the younger children below the age of 12 who are too young to work in the field take care of their even younger siblings at home, while the rest of the family is working.

Living Conditions

The living conditions of farm workers can be appalling. A ranchero song provides a glimpse into their daily life. It is called "How sad it is to hear it rain." It describes how migrant workers and their families live in cardboard houses. It paints a picture of how it is especially sad that sick children who are impacted by disease such as stomach worms are forced "to live in houses of cardboard" that provide little to no protection, especially in a rainstorm.[13]

Furthermore, migrant workers are often housed or live in decrepit trailers, hovels, their cars, wooden shacks, barracks, and poorly constructed and maintained cinderblock houses. Often these quarters are overcrowded with people. They frequently are without running water, electricity, adequate drainage, and can be infested with rats, roaches, parasites, and bugs. Furthermore, sanitation and hygiene levels tend to be substandard in much of the housing. Thus, the risk of picking up various diseases, especially for children, is very high.

Mexican immigrant children inside an old trailer. Alison Wright/CORBIS.

In cities, too, the living conditions of immigrants can be impoverished and tight. For instance, entire large immigrant families who work in low-wage jobs can frequently live huddled in small one-bedroom apartments. Often these families are also cohabitating with extended family members or friends in their flats. In addition, in many instances the bathroom facilities are located outside of the apartment, and they are often communal spaces shared by several families.

Low-wage workers without families in urban areas also often cram into close quarters. They try to save most of their small wages to send home to relatives in their sending societies. For instance, in one case police officers came across a six-by-eight-foot basement room that had 18 people living in it. Several slept directly next to a boiler.[14] This particular case, while in some ways an extreme situation, provides a glimpse of the tight living conditions that some immigrants working in the lower-wage sector experience.

Domestic Labor

Immigrants play a central role in the domestic labor sector. They work in the houses of upper- and middle-class American families, where they help raise the children of their employees, clean, do the laundry, cook meals, go shopping, and fulfill numerous other tasks around the house. These are jobs disproportionately filled by women. Furthermore, some immigrant women work for cleaning and maid services. As employees

Brazilian workers at a construction site. Matt Rainey/Star Ledger/CORBIS.

of these agencies, the workers take care of several different homes a day. The labor can be exhausting. Some also question the long-term health impact that the daily use of cleaning agents that are often laden with aggressive chemicals can have on workers, especially if they are being used by workers for 8 to 14 hours a day.

Construction

There is a strong presence of immigrant workers in the construction industry. They work in all positions in this business. They are carpenters, plumbers, and electricians, and they build drywall, paint, and work various other jobs on construction sites. "According to a study by the Pew Hispanic Center [in 2007], one in five construction workers in the United States is from Latin America. And newly arrived immigrants have taken a third of the country's new construction jobs in the last three years. They are more likely to be undocumented, since it is been difficult to get into the country legally."

The fact that immigrants work for less money—especially those who are in the country illegally—explains in part why they were hired in larger numbers during the housing boom. Lower salaries meant, of course, higher profits for employers and developers. There are, however, also hidden costs that accompany the use of irregular immigrants. These are workers who often have no insurance. When they are sick or injured, they end up in the emergency rooms. These health costs are often passed on as indirect expenses to health care customers who have health insurance and who are forced to pay higher prices for their health care, as well as to tax payers who also carry some of these overheads.[15]

With the housing market crisis that began in the United States in the mid-2000s, the situation for immigrant laborers in construction has been especially tough. Many workers have lost their jobs, but the economic impact of the recession can be felt not only among newcomer families in the United States who lost jobs. Relatives south of the border who have been receiving remittances are also hard hit as they are receiving much less support from their relations in the United States than they did during the boom years.

SMALL BUSINESS OWNERS

There exists a tremendous diversity of immigrant businesses in the United States today, which is aided in part by the fact that many newcomers aspire for economic independence for various reasons. The spirit of entrepreneurship is especially visible in urban areas, where immigrant-run shops and companies provide various services and goods to customers, but small immigrant businesses can be found in small towns, rural areas, and suburbs.

Immigrant enterprise certainly helps in the revitalization of urban areas, which were often previously without enough commerce and economic activity. On the other hand, in certain areas with high concentrations of foreign-born populations, small immigrant businesses are oversaturating the market. This makes it hard for many immigrant-owned businesses to survive due to stiff economic competition. Such conditions can cause economic hardship and bankruptcies, and the turnover rate of immigrant businesses can be high.

A significant presence of small immigrant business can also cause or reinforce racial and ethnic tensions. One can sometimes overhear discriminatory remarks, often spurred by jealousy or ignorance, about foreign-born "outsiders" who look different, speak different languages, and when they speak English, talk with "funny accents." Some people are upset that "these immigrants" are now moving into "their" city neighborhoods, suburbs, or small towns, where they are opening stores, running gas stations, or providing services such as hair salons, manicures/pedicures, or car and electronic repairs. Thus there are some stereotypes and resentment.

Such sentiments can at times flare into outright conflict and violence. During the so called Los Angeles "race riots" of 1992, for example, which were sparked by the beating up of an African-American motorist named Rodney King, Korean American businesses were especially targeted during the violence, arson, and looting. A Korean store owner observed that "[a]fter the Rodney King verdict, the other stores around here were broken into. The windows were smashed. One market down the street was completely looted of everything of value." This was in part due to the fact that some residents of the city had been upset about the killing of an African-American girl by a Korean shop owner two years earlier. They projected their anger about an incident involving one individual onto all Asian shop owners. However, there were general racial and ethnic tensions in the neighborhood before.[16]

Thus, in many cities and neighborhoods the change that immigrants and their businesses bring are not always welcomed. Native-born residents throughout the United States complain about the changing face of their neighborhoods, arguing that their places of current or former residence now look more like they should be in "Asia," "Latin America," the "Middle East," or "Africa" and not in the United States. It is important to emphasize though that many other native-born Americans welcome the diversity. They see the influx of new residents and businesses as a hopeful development that will help in the revitalization efforts of their communities.

Immigrants can be found operating businesses in all fields. They run stores, supermarkets, car repair shops, cleaning shops, import export businesses, electronic shops, hair salons, grocery stores, barber shops, jewelry stores, movie theaters, liquor stores, furniture stores, warehouses, taxi cab companies, restaurants, convenience stores, law firms, tax accountant offices, construction companies, real estate firms, as well as doctor's and dental offices—just to mention a few of their enterprises.

Immigrant businesses provide jobs, investments, and play a central role in daily life. The successful ones can create employment and use their capital to invest either in ethnic communities or in mainstream American society. In case of smaller businesses, they are often family-run enterprises. Families pool their money to make the business possible. In many instances funds are also borrowed from friends and relatives. One Soviet Jewish entrepreneur observed that "I have over 30 relatives . . . and they didn't have a choice [about giving money]. They were my relatives. . . . I just said 'I gotta have it.' "[17] Furthermore, many small businesses require the proprietors to work many hours. A Korean shop owner observes:

I work in this shop fourteen hours a day, seven days a week. My wife works here nine hours a day. The only thing we do is go to church. But even then we can't even go together; one person has to mind the store. I have two children, five and six years old. . . . But I only see them in the morning when I drop them off at preschool before opening our store. By the time I get home at 2:00 a.m. they are already asleep. . . . I have to keep this place open late so that we can pay the rent and service our debts.[18]

This is a typical routine for many small business owners.

Immigrant from Liberia selling her produce in Staten Island, New York. Najlah Feanny/CORBIS.

Furthermore, in many instances family members of the owners often work very long hours for very little money to keep the business afloat. One immigrant explains that his store is open from 8:30 a.m. to 9:00 p.m. seven days a week. Of the 10 people who work at his store, all 10 are family members, which included his wife, his sisters, and their husbands, as well as his father. We "all work together as family. While we are at the store, my mother-in-law watches our children."[19]

In numerous instances, these types of labor arrangements can be exploitative. Relatives can often be compensated inadequately for their work in family businesses. In fact, some economists, sociologists, and labor rights activists have raised concerns and questions about whether many small ethnic enterprises are only sustainable in their operation due to their inadequate compensation and labor manipulation. However, many immigrants see the situation differently. Some prefer to be self-employed because of the independence it provides them, and others prefer to work for a relative due to strong family ties and feelings of loyalty. Some also believe that such employment provides them with greater flexibility and protects them from interacting with mainstream American employers who do not understand their language and culture and who may refuse to hire them or discriminate against them in some way.

Restaurants

Many immigrants enter into the business world by opening a restaurant. In the last few decades, the United States has experienced a dramatic expansion of eating places that offer ethnic or international cuisine. Many communities in the United States have eateries that serve non-American fare. In the most unexpected places at times, one can find, for example, Peruvian, Argentine, Mexican, Dominican, Ethiopian, Nigerian, north and south Indian, Chinese, Mongolian, Lebanese, Afghani, Thai, Vietnamese, or Cambodian restaurants. These countries are only a few among many, and their cuisines have not only popular appeal with ethnic Americans and immigrants, but also with many mainstream Americans.

Stores

There are a wide variety of shops owned by immigrants. These stores cater to diverse clienteles. Many clearly accommodate the tastes of the members of a specific immigrant community and provide a glimpse of that group's culture and habits of daily life. Other businesses, however, target a wider customer base and draw from mainstream society and other immigrant groups.

In stores run by immigrants, for example, hair products for Asian or African consumers can be seen standing next to consumer products like specialty teas, coffees, honey, various types of flour, oils, rice, beans, grains, and cookies. Many immigrant businesses also sell prepackaged and precooked international foods, which appeal to the tastes of the particular group of immigrants to which the specific ethnic business caters. Furthermore, the wide availability of prepackaged ethnic foods is also an indicator that many immigrants have become in some ways "Americanized," but also that our world is becoming increasingly global. Many people around the world increasingly embrace the convenience of a ready-made meal to provide a little relief in a stressful life.

Immigrant stores also stock products such as ketchup made in Hong Kong, canned quail eggs, beautiful African or Asian fabrics or clothing, icons or items of particular religious or spiritual importance, and cookware and dishes that cater to the culinary needs or expectations of a particular immigrant group. Stores often carry tapes of popular music from the sending society. They also at times rent videos and DVDs. This is particularly the case with many South Asian stores, which often have a collection of the latest as well as classic "Bollywood" movies from India.

Such products can also be seen in Latino, Southeast Asian, and African stores, where films from the home region are popular with many customers. They provide a link to a previous life and are often nostalgic reminders of one's country of origin. Yet, like the ethnic restaurants, stores that sell immigrant foods, videos, and music are also becoming popular with at least some mainstream Americans who also like to consume these products. Thus, immigration and globalization is not only having an impact on the daily life of immigrants, but also on that of native-born Americans.

Many of the immigrant-owned stores also feature European products and goods, popularized by Western powers when these nations colonized areas around the globe during the nineteenth and the first half of the twentieth century. Today many of these foreign products and foods have become part of the consumption patterns in many parts of the non-Western world. They continue to remain popular consumer items with immigrants when they come to Western countries like the United States.

Fresh products can also be found in many immigrant stores. As in most mainstream American supermarkets, chicken legs can be found alongside other meat products, such as beef, sometimes pork, or, to mainstream American customers, more unusual items such as tripe, liver, or chicken feet. Some businesses sell fresh, smoked, or frozen fish, and other seafood items. Others sell vegetables, fruits, and herbs. Many items that are being sold are familiar to Western customers, such as bananas, oranges, tomatoes, onions, salads, or avocados. Some of the fruits, vegetables, and herbs might appear alien or unfamiliar, however, such as the leaves of the Taro plant, which are sold especially in Indian or Southeast Asian stores. These leaves are used to make Patra, a popular vegetarian dish in the Gujarat region of India. Cambodians also use the leaves in their cuisine.

Immigrants run many of the convenience stores and gas stations in urban and suburban areas. These businesses cater to mainstream American and newcomer customers alike. They sell numerous regular staples such as packaged name-brand groceries, canned food, milk, soft drinks, coffee, juices, and candy just to mention a few of their items. Often they sell coffee to go, cigarettes, as well as scratch and lottery tickets.

BUSINESS AND THE CORPORATE WORLD

Immigrants can also be in the upper echelons of the business world. *Forbes* magazine writes that according "to the National Venture Capital Association, immigrants ... have started" about "one in four of all U.S. public companies that have been venture-backed" in the last two decades or so. These creators of corporations include Andrew Grove, a cofounder of Intel, Sergey Brin, a cofounder of Google, Jerry Yang, cofounder of Yahoo, Liz Claiborne, founder of Liz Claiborne Inc., and Andreas Bechtolsheim and Vinod Khosla, cofounders of Sun Microsystems.[20]

In addition, there are numerous foreign-born chief executive officers (CEOs) who run major American corporations today. The online magazine Slate.com observes:

In many ways, this trend makes complete sense. Big American businesses—like Alcoa, Pepsi, Coke, and AIG—are already global businesses. Based on data from 238 members of the Standard & Poor's 500 Index, S&P analyst Howard Silverblatt found that the typical member of the index generated 44.2 percent of its sales outside the United States in 2006. And the bigger the company—and the more it has saturated the U.S. market—the more important it is to have a CEO who is comfortable operating around the world.[21]

As the business world is becoming more and more interconnected, this trend is likely to continue in the future.

Immigrants can be found working at all levels of the corporate world. They play a pivotal role in helping the United States boost its number of start-up companies. While many of the immigrants who began companies are foreign born, a good number of them were educated in management, sciences, engineering, and the liberal arts at American colleges and universities. After receiving their degrees, they decided to pursue business opportunities and careers in the United States. Sun Microsystems, Google, and Intel are only some of the major companies that were created with the aid of foreign-born founders, but immigrants have helped to build thousands of small companies that push for electronic, medical, and biotechnological innovation and production and that provide a multitude of services. These businesses have created numerous well-paying jobs—both for foreign-born and for native-born Americans.

Some immigrants in the business world have a "rags to riches" story. An individual's marketable idea and savvy can lead to the creation of a booming business. In most other cases, hard work and determination can lead an individual of relative modest means to open up a successful and lucrative business. This often means putting in 15 to 16 hours a day, working six to seven days a week, pouring one's heart and soul into a business, which is done out of hope that the monetary resources raised by this endeavor will improve one's future.

Immigrants work at all levels of corporate America. They are not only CEOs who direct huge multinational companies or are creators of businesses, but they also work as mid-level managers. Others work as scientists in labs developing various products ranging from medicines to foods, beauty products, detergents, and numerous other products. Many also work as engineers in the corporate world. They develop new technologies, computer programs, machineries, weapon systems, and create new inventions. Given the nature of the international business world, some corporate employees and their families lead transnational lives due to corporate relocations. Some have lived in various countries, and they frequently travel around the world for business or to stay connected with family and friends. They are often fluent in two or more languages.

The global and transnational implications of business play themselves out on other levels as well. In March 2008, for example, the Kenyan newspaper the *Daily Nation* reported on a Kenyan-born businessman living in the United States who successfully started a private nursing company, which had just recently successfully merged with a large educational firm. The fact that this story is covered in a Kenyan newspaper in many ways underscores the global nature of business. Furthermore, it points to the transnational connections that migration is creating between different corners of the world and the expressions of pride that a sending society feels when one of its native sons or daughters is doing well in a foreign country. This story provides a glimpse of the global and transnational impact that an individual's professional life can have.[22]

CONSUMERS

Immigrants are not only active in the U.S. economy as workers, investors, store owners, business leaders, and innovators, but they also play a role as consumers. Immigrants certainly frequent ethnic and immigrant businesses and stores, but as alluded to in Chapter 1, it is also clear that they shop at smaller non-ethnic-oriented businesses, supermarkets, large chain stores, and shopping malls. They eat at ethnic restaurants that feature cuisine from their home countries, but many also have developed a taste for American-style food, eating at smaller independently owned American establishments, big chain restaurants, or at eateries that feature ethnic cuisine from different immigrant groups. Many go to movie theaters, can be seen as spectators at sporting events, and consume a variety of other forms of entertainment.

The expressed desire to become homeowners or the pride of being a homeowner is also a defining feature of many immigrants. Certainly, the rate of homeownership is not as high among immigrants as it is among native-born Americans. The newcomers face many more hurdles on their path to becoming homeowners. They are also often more susceptible to losing their homes in tough economic times. It is much harder for foreign-born Americans or recent immigrants to establish credit, which makes it more difficult for them to obtain a mortgage.

Immigrants often do not have the help of parents or grandparents, who could provide financial support for a mortgage, as this is often the case with many native-born, middle-class American families. Thus, in 2000 about 48 percent of immigrants were homeowners, compared to about two-thirds of the American population in general. Yet, many attempt to become homeowners as soon as they can financially manage to do so—saving as much money as they can to move toward this goal. First-generation immigrants buy homes in cities, but also in more recent years they have opted to buy homes in suburban as well as in rural areas.

Many immigrants also remain economically involved with their birthplaces. As we will see in more detail in Chapter 3, many economically support their families in their homelands with financial contributions

Immigrant shopping at a discount store. Janet Jarman/CORBIS.

such as remittances. Furthermore, some newcomers also own or plan to own real estate in their countries of origin. They are buying or building houses, or they own apartments. During visits to their sending societies, many bring gifts or cash for relatives or friends. Many also send packages and letters throughout the year to family members and other close relations. These mailings are often filled with goods and sometimes cash. Immigrants also use banks or Western Union, or they have more informal financial networks through which they can send money to loved ones abroad.

THE NEW SLAVERY

There is also a darker side to migrants in the American and the global economy. While slavery has been officially outlawed in the United States since the nineteenth century, it still occurs in pockets throughout the United States and the world. In America work conditions that can be characterized as slave labor exist in some sweatshops that produce garments, in some small-scale manufacturers, in parts of the agricultural sector, and in the area of domestic work. Sexual trafficking and prostitution is another area where slave labor can occur. Immigrants are often the most likely victims of this labor system.

To use the terminology of "slaves" and "slavery" to describe modern abusive labor relations is not without controversy. Yet, the way that some employers in the United States and around the world use their workers perfectly fits this description. It is estimated that there are about 27 million slaves around the world. These figures are based on approximations, as exact numbers are hard to come by. A slave is a person who is being obligated to work. This can be done by force or through fraud. Furthermore, a slave receives no compensation for her or his services beyond what is required for their subsistence.[23]

In the last few decades there have been occasional media reports about the use of slave labor throughout the United States. "With an average term of enslavement lasting at least three years," writes the journalist E. Benjamin Skinner in his book *A Crime So Monstrous: Face to Face with Modern Slavery,* "there are now some 50,000 slaves in the United States. Most victims come from Asia or Mexico, although several thousand are Eastern European, Central American, or African. U.S. officials have discovered slaves from over three dozen countries."[24]

Slave labor is illegally utilized in a variety of sectors in the American economy. It is estimated that about 1 in 10 of the enslaved persons in the United States works in the agricultural sector. Many slaves are of Mexican origin, trapped in a system of agricultural debt bondage from which they cannot escape. In Florida, which has a $62-billion strong agricultural industry, the police and outreach groups have located hundreds of slaves—likely to be only the tip of the iceberg.

As in other nations around the world, slave labor is also being utilized in the sex industry in the United States. The brothels and massage parlors that draw on enslaved prostitutes are often run by Asian criminal gangs. One such establishment was found on the upper floors of a building in New York City. During a police raid, 30 enslaved Thai prostitutes were located there. The women were trapped by barred windows, and various secured gates denied them access to the streets. The brothel owner, who had close ties with a criminal gang, had bought each woman for thousands of dollars and charged them for room and board. The prostitutes were forced to work from 11 a.m. to 4 a.m. They worked seven days a week and were sold by the hour. This incident is not an isolated case of migrant slave labor in the sex industry, however. Immigration authorities believe that more than 250 brothels in the United States make use of trafficked women.[25]

Furthermore, some employers in the sweatshops of the garment industry use slave labor. These clothing manufacturers can still be found in many urban areas in the United States. In some instances, the workers are imprisoned. Their living and employment conditions are horrific. They work very long days and under horrendously uncomfortable conditions. Their living quarters are crammed, often squalid, and frequently in the same place where they work. Time and again, there is limited access to bathrooms and the outside world.

On occasion the local, national, and international media report on the use of slaves as domestic workers in the United States. The unfortunate individuals who get trapped into these situations often face physical and psychological abuse. The victims of such cruelty are from wide national, ethnic, and racial backgrounds. The *restaveks*, a term used for children that work as slaves in Haiti, are one group that has been given some attention. While their use is widely reported in the Caribbean nation, they are also being employed as domestic slaves by some Haitian families who are living in America. In late September 1999, for instance, police freed a 12-year-old child from a suburban Miami home. Apparently the Haitian family had purchased the girl in Haiti and had brought her to the United States. She was forced to keep the house clean, eat trash, had no bed to sleep in, was sexually abused, and suffered from a venereal disease.[26]

There are also sometimes reports of the use of slave labor in the industrial sector. In 2002, for example, an industrialist outside of Tulsa, Oklahoma, got into legal trouble for employing Indian workers. He claimed that they had come to the United States as part of a job training program. In fact, they were treated and used as slave laborers, working long hours under horrific conditions, and for unfair wages.[27] One witness, a migrant laborer who had worked in various parts of the world, described the living conditions of the slaves in an appalled tone:

The rooms were filled with beds so close together that it was difficult to walk between them. The top bunk of the bunk beds was within two and a half feet of the ceiling. The dorm was only a very small house. The entire space, including a garage, which we utilized as a common room, was approximately 1,500 square feet. There was no carpet on the floors. The only place for all of our belongings was in our luggage underneath our bunks. We had no private place for our belongings. The dorm provided no privacy. It had four showers, two urinals, and two toilets. We had one place to wash our hands between thirty men.... The dorm was also equipped with only one washing machine and one dryer.

Initially, there were no tables to sit at to eat. After one week a small table for about eight people was provided. Most of us had to stand or sit on the floor in the garage while we ate.[28]

This quote provides a glimpse of the daily life and the generally poor living conditions of immigrant slave laborers in the United States.

Irregular immigrants are particularly vulnerable to exploitation as slaves. The system of new slavery traps and targets particularly the weak and young because they are the least likely to resist. They often do not know the language and the legal system of the country that they have been brought too. Furthermore, and even on those occasions where the slaves could escape their situation, they are often too intimidated to do so. They are afraid to surrender to the authorities for fear that they might be deported or punished, or that officials might be corrupt, a reality that many migrants expect because that is the situation in some of their sending societies.

Slave labor occurs in the United States as one journalist aptly writes "in out-of-the-way places that are ... beyond most Americans 'cognitive map.' They're hidden down country roads and in culturally remote immigrant communities, where law enforcement is lax and modern ideas of 'human rights' are sketchy."[29] The immigrant slaves lead the most dreadful daily lives.

NOTES

1. Virginia Yans-McLaughlin, ed., *Immigration Reconsidered: History, Sociology, and Politics* (New York: Oxford University Press, 1990).

2. Khalid Koser, *International Migration: A Very Short Introduction* (New York: Oxford University Press, 2007), 10.

3. Mark Krikorian, "Debate: Are Illegal Immigrants Good for the U.S. Economy?" *New York Times: Upfront*, September 1, 2008, 28.

4. Walter Ewing, "Debate: Are Illegal Immigrants Good for the U.S. Economy?" *New York Times: Upfront*, September 1, 2008, 28.

5. Neeraj Kaushal, Cordelia Reimers, and David Reimers, "Immigrants and the Economy," in *The New Americans: A Guide to Immigration Since 1965*, ed. Mary Waters and Reed Ueda (Cambridge, MA: Harvard University Press, 2007), 176–188.

6. Kaushal et al., 178–179.

7. Yans-McLaughlin, 10.

8. Kaushal et al., 184–185.

9. Eric Schlosser, *Fast Food Nation: The Dark Side of the All American Meal* (New York: Houghton Mifflin Company, 2001), 169–176, 172.

10. Schlosser, 169–176.

11. Schlosser, 177.

12. Schlosser, 176–178.

13. John Annerion, *Dead in Their Tracks: Crossing America's Desert Borderlands* (New York: Basic Books, 2003), 111.

14. Jeff Struck, "Brazilian Natives Charged in Document Forgery Scheme," *Lowell Sun*, May 3, 2002.

15. Bianca Vazquez Toness, "Counting on Immigration, Part 3," *wbur.org*, http://www.wbur.org/news/2007/72346_20071114.asp (accessed November 16, 2007).

16. "A Korean American's Bitter Life in the United States, 1984–1992," in *Major Problems in American Immigration and Ethnic History*, ed. Jon Gjerde (New York: Houghton Mifflin Company, 1998), 462–463; Nancy Abelmann and John Lie, *Blue Dreams: Korean Americans and the Los Angeles Riots* (Cambridge, MA: Harvard University Press, 1995).

17. Quoted in Ivan Light and Steven Gold, *Ethnic Economies* (San Francisco: Academic Press, 2000), 144.

18. "A Korean American's Bitter Life in the United States," 461–462.

19. Cha Ok Kim, "The Peddler," in *The New Americans an Oral History: Immigrants and Refugees in the United States Today,* ed. Al Santoli (New York: Viking, 1988), 165.

20. Mary Crane, "Out of China," May 29, 2007, *Forbes.com*, http://www.forbes.com/2007/05/21/outsourcing-entrepreneurs-immigrants-oped-cx_mc_0522entrepreneurs.html (accessed April 18, 2008).

21. Daniel Gross, "Send Us Your Tired, Your Poor, Your Business Executives: Why Are Big American Companies Hiring Foreign-Born CEOs?" August 17, 2007, *Slate.com*. http://www.slate.com/id/2172346/ (accessed May 29, 2008).

22. Enock Wambua, "US-based Kenyan Businessman Joins the Big League," March 30, 2008, *Nationmedia.com*. http://www.nationmedia.com/dailynation/printpage.asp?newsid=119558 (accessed April 15, 2008).

23. Kevin Bales, *Disposable People: New Slavery in the Global Economy,* Second Edition (Berkeley: University of California Press, 2004), 1–33.

24. E. Benjamin Skinner, *A Crime So Monstrous: Face-to-Face with Modern Slavery* (New York: Free Press, 2008), 265.

25. Bales, 70; Skinner, 265–266.

26. Skinner, 8–9.

27. John Bowe, *Nobodies: Modern American Slave Labor and the Dark Side of the New Global Economy* (New York: Random House, 2007), 89–150.

28. Bowe, 109.

29. Bowe, XVIII.

3

THE TIES THAT BIND: FAMILY LIFE AND IDENTITY

Family plays a central role in the daily life of many immigrants and features prominently in their social, cultural, and economic existence. Family and relatives and the obligations and reciprocal relations one has with their close kin shape and define, at least in part, the identities of numerous newcomers to the United States.

The family fulfills various functions in the daily life of many immigrants. For example, it can be a source of economic obligations. Having to provide food, shelter, and financial assistance to one's spouse, children, parents, and sometimes extended family such as aunts, uncles, or cousins either in the United States or in one's country of origin, is a reality for many foreign-born residents. At the same time, relatives can also provide assistance or a security blanket in tough economic times, offer financial support and help with labor when opening up a business, or help raise one's children.

Family performs an important social role in daily life. Intimate familial relations can provide joy, emotional stability, and support, but they can also lead to conflict. This can be observed during intergenerational interactions between parents and their children or grandparents and their grandkids.

More so than any previous group of newcomers, the most recent generation of immigrants has been influenced by the processes of globalization and by transnational connections. These often reach far beyond the borders of the United States. This is not to say that immigrants in the nineteenth or early twentieth century were not connected to their countries of origin. But in a period of mass travel at comparatively low prices and high speed, and with improved means of mass communication through phone services and the Internet, global and transnational links today have become much easier to maintain than a century ago. Improved travel and communication have had a significant impact on helping immigrants maintain their relationships with their family members outside of the United States, which helps to shape, reinforce, and influence the personal, family, community, and national identities of many immigrants.

THE FAMILY: THE LOCAL AND THE TRANSNATIONAL

The daily life of many of today's immigrants takes place in the United States as well as abroad. Like people in mainstream society, many new immigrants live regular lives. They work, shop, and go to religious worship. They raise their children and send them to school. Immigrants live in cities, towns, suburbs, and rural areas all over the United States. They have made these places their homes.

Still, the lives of many immigrants often reach far past the national borders of the United States. Some newcomers, for example, own real estate and businesses outside of the United States. They shop, invest, or support social or welfare programs in their countries of origin. Some immigrants find spouses in their country of birth or, in some instances, in one of the immigrant communities from the same sending society, but in a different country. Others send their children back to their sending societies to be raised there by family members such as grandparents or aunts and uncles. These connections and interactions with home countries and with family networks outside of an immigrant's place of residence are described as transnational.

Transnational and National Family Ties

Transnational family ties and networks play an important part in the daily lives of many immigrants. Many of them travel back and forth between their current places of residence and their countries of origin. Some also visit family members who have immigrated to other parts of the world.

Migration and immigration in the post–World War II world has become a truly global and transnational phenomenon. The intensifying processes of the last few decades mean that we are living in what some scholars have called an "age of migration."[1] International global migration continues to have an impact on economics, cultures, and politics, and it creates ethnic diversity in many countries around the world. Yet, at the same time, the international movement of people can create close transnational relationships between migrants and their sending societies.

One scholar observes that the "proliferation" of "long-term transnational ties challenges conventional notions about assimilation of immigrants into host countries and about migration's impact on sending-country life." This point is likely to remain relevant as a growing number of immigrants are likely to continue to stay connected not only with their country of residence but also with their sending societies. They are living transnational lives between two and sometimes even more places. Many immigrants "are not bounded by national borders. They do not shift their loyalties and participatory energies from one country to another. Instead, they are integrated, to varying degrees, into the countries that receive them, at the same time that they remain connected to the countries they leave behind."[2]

Many newcomers see international travel as an essential way to maintain close ties with their families, but it can also lead to the creation of new relationships. A West African immigrant from the Ivory Coast, for example, tells the story of how he met his current wife. She is also from the Ivory Coast. The two, however, began their romantic engagement in France. There they were introduced while he was visiting his Ivorian cousin, who is a French citizen.[3] A young Vietnamese American relates a similar experience:

I just went back to Vietnam for vacation. . . . I met this girl and I hung out with her for two weeks. . . . My parents knew this girl already. I think they set this up behind my back. So I asked her to be my girlfriend . . . and she said "Yes." And she also said that she wanted me, or my parents to go meet her parents. . . . So I said, "Okay, I will do that." So the two parents sat down and talked. . . . After that my mother came over to me and said, "Okay, I think you should buy some jewelry for her." There needs to be a promise gift. . . . I bought her a promise ring, necklace, earrings and everything. . . . I call it a semi-engagement.[4]

These are not unusual or exceptional occurrences. The meeting of spouses or potential future marriage partners can frequently happen through transnational ties and connections. These relationships can further strengthen the links between an immigrant and the sending society and culture and can reinforce ethnic or hyphen identities.

Weddings can be transnational affairs as well. A young Indian-American woman who by the time of the interview had been in the United States for about 10 years explains:

I've been to India twice, and a lot of times my family goes back because of family stuff. My cousins wedding . . . even though they're in the U.S. . . . It just feels better if you have an Indian wedding in India because you have all the traditional stuff and everything. So that's why I've been back, once for my cousin's wedding and once for my sister's wedding even though they were both here.

The interviewee, too, would contemplate a wedding in India in the future, and she still shops for her saris and many other items while visiting her birthplace.

Such transnational weddings can be elaborate celebrations. The woman describes her experience in India:

First of all it was a five day event. The first day is when family first starts coming in, just different family from India. . . . The second day . . . there is a [henna] ceremony . . . when the ladies just get together and everybody gets that done on their hands. The third night was basically like a dance night, but it's Indian traditional dancing. . . . So that's the third night and everybody just gets together from the girl's side and the groom's side. And they have food there. And the fourth day is when everything starts coming together. They have a ceremony at the girl's place separate from the one going on for the boys at his place. So that happens on the fourth day, a totally separate ceremony for the individual families. And then on the fifth day is the real wedding. But it was really big . . . my sister, she was the first girl to get married in my family, so it was a big deal.

Globalization and outside influences also have left their mark on India. Traditionally, the bride's family carried all or most of the costs related to the wedding. These days, however, families frequently split the expenses of the celebration.[5]

To keep stronger connections to their homelands and to their families, some foreign-born residents in the United States also own houses or apartments in their countries of origin. It provides them a place to stay when they visit. It also keeps them connected. Some immigrants dream about returning to their homelands when they retire and hope to live in that real estate. Others use their houses and apartments as an investment for rental income to support themselves through retirement. Again others plan to spend part of the year in their sending societies for extended stays, visits, or vacations.

Such plans frequently work out, but not always, as people's agendas and plans tend to change over time. An Armenian-American woman who had purchased an apartment in Armenia with her husband explains that "originally we bought it so that when we retired we could spend half the year there, half the year here. But with the grandchild, it's difficult. And besides, both my daughter and son-in-law, both of them are teachers. So during the year we can't go there. We're taking care of the baby. And so it stays until summer."[6]

Other immigrants pull through with their plans to leave, but then can change their mind once they have left. A Puerto Rican woman spoke of her experience of returning to the island where she was born. "A couple of years ago I went back to Puerto Rico. I was there for 10 years and then came back." She said she missed the city where she lived in the United States, "even though I was in my own culture. I found it very difficult and different. Finally I decided I can't take it any longer. I am going back."[7] Thus, and as these quotes suggests, not wanting to leave loved ones behind such as family and friends, as well as numerous other obligations, emotional attachments, familiarity with the United States and one's place of residence, various responsibilities, all these, as well as several other reasons, can at times be an impediment for immigrants in their plans to lead transnational lives or to return to their places of birth.

Furthermore, immigrants do not only travel internationally to see family members, but they also sojourn throughout the United States and sometimes Canada to visit relatives who, like them, have immigrated to North America. As family plays a central role in the daily life of many, it is important to connect with relatives even if they live halfway or all the way across the country or continent. Travel in the United States can also happen for religious reasons. Some immigrants, for example, travel throughout the United States and Canada following their religious leaders when they come to visit North America from their sending societies.

Family members from outside the United States also sometimes come to visit their relatives in America. With the growing concern among federal officials about irregular immigration as well as with rising security concerns since the terrorist attacks on September 11 and the stricter enforcement of immigration laws that resulted from these developments, these kind of visits have become harder to host. This observation seems to apply especially to people who have family members in Middle Eastern countries in specific, and in developing countries in general.

It is important to underscore that the transnational implications of immigration also have an impact on daily life in sending societies. Thus, immigration does not only influence the receiving country, but it also changes the sending society. These influences and transformations can be economic and political, but also often social and cultural. We will further develop some of these issues below.

Travel and Identities

Visits to sending societies often reinforce the realization among immigrants that their experience and their lives in the United States have changed them. Some have come to firmly believe that the United States has become their home. An immigrant of Vietnamese descent who had arrived in the United States as a refugee in the early 1980s, for example, reported:

Since I left [Vietnam] in 1981 I went back once. . . . Before that trip, when I talked to people, I used the term, "my country," when I referred to Vietnam. After that trip I realized that home is here . . . America. Vietnam is where I came from, but I realized my future is here. After that trip I became more American than ever. . . . It's funny. . . . I realized that America is much more comfortable for my lifestyle. The longer you live in America you realize that you know more about American culture, language, laws, business, everything else, and the less you know about where you came from.[8]

For other immigrants matters are not as straightforward. Visiting their home country can leave them confused about their identity. A Cambodian immigrant, who also came to the United States as a refugee, expressed his mixed and complex feelings on the issue of belonging:

I know I am an American. Personally, it didn't click with me until I went to Cambodia. The thing is . . . I can't answer the question because I don't know who I am. Reason is my mom went to Cambodia and she was with me and was showing me. She said, "See that tree over there; when I was young I use to climb that tree. . . . I used to do this and I used to do that." Now, when it was my turn, I went to Cambodia, for the first year I did not go to my home town. I have no recollection or remember where I was born. I know I was born somewhere in Cambodia but I don't know [where]. I don't have any memories like this is where my house was. I remember a lot of the Thai border and the camps—I lived there for six or seven years. Now I am here. [At the same time] I am not an American either. It is almost like I am floating from one place to the next. I feel comfortable but I am not at peace to say Cambodia is my home or the U.S. is my home. It is really hard to actually know where you are. I don't think I can answer until one day I can say that this is who I am or this is what I am.[9]

As these comments demonstrate, traveling to one's place of birth can provide more clarity to some immigrants about who they are, while to others it can create more confusion.

Ethnicity, race, and how an immigrant is perceived by as well as how she or he sees herself or himself fitting into society certainly complicates issues of identity. The statements of an immigrant from Cambodia provide a glimpse of the complexity of this matter:

I can say I am a Cambodian American because I was naturalized and my daughter is born here and she is an American just like anybody else. But is she? She can say she is an American. But [then] somebody else can say you are not, you [are] Cambodian. I guess it goes back to who that person you are dealing with is. No matter what, I am going to be Cambodian. It doesn't matter where I physically live or where I go. I am Cambodian. I am here legally, I am a naturalized citizen. I am an American. Yet, the inner self of me is saying I am Cambodian. I can eat American food and I can adapt. But you can't get the Cambodian out of me. You can put a lot of stuff in me but I don't think you can get the Cambodian out of me; just like you can't get the American out of someone else, same thing with my kids. They can justify it by saying I am born here. I can speak the language and it is my home. So I am an American. But she has to believe that.[10]

Thus, for every generation of immigrants issues of identity are complex and shaped by societal forces, outside views, and personal beliefs.

It would be wrong to assume that all immigrants lead transnational lives. While certainly many go to visit their sending societies frequently, others, for various political, economic, or social reasons, have not traveled or travel far less. Many are quite unfamiliar with the transformations that have occurred in their countries of origin and sometimes have not spent time there in years and in some cases even decades. One interviewee revealed his surprise after visiting the Vietnamese island where he had spent his early childhood:

Fifteen years ago the island was a sleepy little town. No road had been paved, houses made out of wood and grass, not many brick houses, no sewer system, no traffic light, no flush toilets, or running water. But now it is very different. All of that has changed. The island has turned to commercialism. Houses are changed, roads paved, hotels built and being built at the moment. Westerners everywhere and Western money is coming in to invest. Land is worth as much as U.S. real estate now. So that is a huge change. Then another huge change that I saw was running water and electricity, it's everywhere. Traffic lights and also Internet . . . satellite dishes. . . . I was shocked.[11]

The processes of globalization, and the fast-pace change that they can bring to some societies, can be hard enough to grasp for the people who are actually living through the changes. It is even more of a surprise to an immigrant who returns to his or her country of origin after being away for 10 or 20 years.

Keeping in Touch

Immigrants have devised a variety of ways to keep in touch with family members internationally. A young Polish American woman in her twenties, who had come to the United States in the 1990s, explained that she and her family communicate in various ways with their relatives and friends in Eastern Europe. She said that she keeps in touch by using "IM in Polish and e-mail." Her parents, on the other hand, use phone cards to call family members. "There are certain companies that my parents use. I'm different," she explains, "I use the Internet. That's just faster, easier to keep in touch."[12]

Today, arguably the most used means of international communication by immigrant families is the phone. Many use regular land lines. This can become expensive, though, as phone companies charge high prices for international calls. Thus, there has been a growing industry of phone card providers. They can be bought for cheap online. Some companies advertise that certain countries can be called for less than a cent per minute, most countries for less than eight cents a minute. Advertisements for international phone cards can also be seen in many stores in immigrant neighborhoods around the Western world where they are sold. The images on the cards are revealing. Phone cards marketing for calls to Africa sometimes show a picture of a lion, and those to Asia can show famous buildings or structures like the Taj Mahal, the Chinese wall, or Angkor Wat. Some immigrants also use computer video phone systems like Skype, which allow them to call their loved ones at very inexpensive rates, but require both sides to have access to a computer and the Internet. This relatively easy and inexpensive ability to call provides many immigrants with a way to stay in touch with family members around the globe.

The Internet and the information revolution of recent years introduced myriad ways to communicate. These developments have a significant impact on how some immigrants keep in touch with loved ones.

Above, we have already alluded to Internet phone systems. Furthermore, e-mail, instant messaging, social networking sites like Facebook or MySpace, blogging, and twittering, among several others, have become ways of communication. Even though in many developing countries the availability of home computers and Internet access is limited, Internet cafes are often widely available in areas with higher population densities, which allow those left behind to communicate with relatives in the United States and Europe. As the above-mentioned quote makes clear, however, and while this observation certainly does not apply exclusively, different generations of immigrants tend to use different ways of communication.

Satellite and cable television is another outlet that is available to many new immigrants to stay in touch with developments in their sending societies and to provide a link to their native culture. Many cable providers, for an additional charge, offer international television stations that provide exclusive programming from one country. Thus, for example, a Cambodian immigrant can access a Cambodian television channel, while an immigrant from France can watch French television. Furthermore, given the growing Latino population in the United States, and especially in urban areas, there are now often several television stations even in one media market that broadcast exclusively in Spanish. Accessing these stations does not require a cable subscription, but they can be received by using a regular outside or indoor antenna. There has also been considerable growth in other "ethnic" media such as newspapers, magazines, or radio stations that cater their programming toward particular immigrant groups.

Transnational Good Works

Some newcomers stay involved and connected with their homelands in other ways. Many immigrants decide to give back to their sending societies. For instance, some combine their monetary resources and fund projects in their countries of origin, such as care for the elderly, scholarships for students, as well as maintenance and renovation of public spaces and churches. Immigrants are involved in public work projects, building health care facilities, wells for clean water, or in some cases universities. Others provide natural disaster assistance during such events like the Asian tsunami or during major earthquakes. These efforts at good works are not exclusively reserved to immigrants' places of birth. During Hurricane Katrina, for example, several immigrant groups were involved with the disaster assistance in Louisiana and Mississippi.

Financial Support and Remittances

Some immigrants come to the United States with the understanding that they will have to support family members in their sending societies. Others receive requests and sometimes even pressures from their family members in their countries of origin to support them. One immigrant who came to the United States from West Africa reports his experience. "Almost every other month someone would call to ask for help. And we do it because we believe that we have a little more than they do," he said. "So we don't hesitate to go half way to help out. Sometimes we go all the way but most of the time we go half way. We have needs also so we cannot go all the way all the time."[13] Support to loved ones in sending societies can be sent in the form of wired money, but also in kind, in goods such as clothing or electronics, and, as we have seen above, in various forms of good works.

Immigrants also at times complain that family members in their sending societies have a false sense of reality about their daily life in the United States. While many immigrants generally state that they are better off living in America compared to many of their family members who stay behind and that they are grateful and appreciative of having had the opportunity to have come to the United States, they also underscore that they still face many hardships, financial responsibilities, and insecurities. It can be somewhat frustrating to have to frequently comply with relatives' expectations for support. This can create strong pressures, which play themselves out in complex emotions of being asked for too much while, at the same time, often feeling guilty for not doing enough for one's extended family network.

Furthermore, there are times when one feels obligated to bring expensive gifts when traveling back to one's sending society. Many family members in the non-Western world often have a distorted image of the United States. Many perceive America as a land of "milk and honey," with endless resources, where everybody is rich. Some immigrants observe with frustration that many of their relations do not realize how hard they have to work to make ends meet in the United States.

The reasons why immigrants support family members in their country of origin certainly vary, often depending on an individual's background and views, but various cultural assumptions and values about responsibilities towards one's family and kin influence the decision of many newcomers. The West-African immigrant quoted above explains that "your contribution defines you; your contribution to the community, to your family, and to your extended family. What you do defines you as a person. If someone is in need and you don't participate then you are a nobody. That is how we define a person. As Africans we have to live to that level, live to that expectation."[14] Such feelings of familial duty are especially influencing the first generation of immigrants to the United States, who frequently feel strong bonds with their place of birth. However, commitments of such nature are often waning with later generations, which lack the strong ties of their parents or grandparents.

The financial relationship between immigrant and home country can be quite standardized, meaning that many immigrants send monthly, sometimes bimonthly, or weekly payments to family members. Economists and sociologists describe such a transfer of funds as remittances. The economies of many countries in the non-Western world depend on the remittances sent by migrant laborers based in the United States or in other Western countries. Some Latin American economies especially rely on remittances sent from the United States. In 2007, immigrants wired $66.5 billion to Latin America.

While Asian economies received about $114 billion in remittances in 2006, in per capita terms the money sent back by immigrant workers still played a much more important role in Latin American economies. An estimated 20 million families in the region are believed to receive regular payments from relatives abroad. In 2007, for example, Mexican immigrants in the United States send almost $24 billion to their country of origin. According to estimates of the Inter-American Development Bank (IDB), Guyana received 43 percent of its gross domestic product (GDP) through remittances, Haiti 35 percent, Honduras 25 percent, El Salvador 18 percent, Jamaica 18 percent, and Mexico about 2 percent to 3 percent.

In many ways, funds sent to Latin American countries from immigrants in the United States have an impact on the daily life there, as they help to alleviate poverty and provide the basis for moderate business investments. Experts, however, also point out that the positive impact of remittances as tools of economic development should not be overstated. There

The Western Union Office in Passaic, New Jersey. Immigrants in the United States often use such offices to wire money to relatives abroad. AP Photo/Mike Derer.

is some debate about the effectiveness of remittances in alleviating inequality and poverty levels. They certainly assist many families and communities. Many immigrants point out that they believe that the money they send home to their family has a positive impact. It enables their relations to buy material goods they would otherwise not be able to afford.

In many cases, the outside flow of cash also allows families in developing countries to eat better and gain access to education and health care. At the same time, as any alert traveler or person that has spent some time in developing countries can attest, the inflow of outside funds can also create a class rift within communities, where those who have relations abroad become more affluent and those who do not remain stuck in poverty. Such developments can lead to jealousy within communities. Seeing their families lose status in comparison with their neighbors can spur some individuals to migrate voluntarily. In other cases, it can lead disadvantaged families to pressure one or more family members to undertake the often arduous and dangerous trip to the Western world.

Research demonstrates that at the national level the evidence that shows the influence of remittances on reducing poverty is not as straightforward. It can reinforce economic dependency of nation-states on these outside sources of income. Remittances generally do not help the poorest, and they also do not reduce social inequality. In fact, an over reliance by economies on these payments at levels of 25 percent or more of the GDP might simply be dangerous.[15] Remittances can change patterns of daily life in sending societies and lead to greater dependency.

A sociologist who has studied the impact of economic remittances sent by relatives in the United States on families in the Dominican Republic observes that even though many there "have more income and live better than they did before large scale migration began, few have achieved this through their own labor. Instead they have grown accustomed to greater comfort, and they covet even more, as their ability to accomplish this on their own grows weaker."[16]

Reliance on remittances creates a dependency on the outside world and makes communities particularly vulnerable to fluctuations in the global economy. Officials with the Inter-American Development Bank argue that with the global economic downturn in 2008, remittances to Latin America have shrunk noticeably. They describe this development as a worrying trend. BBC News writes that the "bank estimates that about 600,000 Mexicans did not receive remittances as a result of the turndown last year. Normally a worker sends between $100 and $300 back home every month." Many Mexicans who worked as construction workers lost their jobs due to the housing market crisis of 2007 and 2008 and the proceeding decline in home construction in the United States.[17]

There are a variety of other factors that influence the flow of remittances sent by immigrants in the United States to their sending societies. The crackdown by federal authorities, as well as by some states and local communities, on undocumented workers that followed 9/11, as well as the uncertainty about new immigration laws, certainly has led some immigrants to leave the country voluntarily. Others, after detainment, are being sent back to their countries of origin. Such developments undermine immigrants' ability to send back funds to their relatives, which can have a potentially harmful impact on these individual's families as well on those Latin American economies that have come to depend heavily on the remittances of migrant workers.

For instance, in 2007 and 2008, fearing deportation, being discouraged by the weakening dollar in relation to the Brazilian currency, the reais, and drawn by a strengthening Brazilian economy, a growing number of Brazilian immigrants left the United States to return to their home nation. These factors led to a decline of remittances sent to Brazil from the United States during that period. In addition, due to the declining value of the dollar in 2008, and due to fears of a crackdown on irregular immigrants by U.S. federal authorities, a growing number of Latin American migrants from countries like Ecuador and Bolivia were increasingly heading to the European Union, especially Spain. They pursued this strategy in the hope of getting paid in a stronger currency to send home in form of remittances and in hopes of facing a less hostile political climate with regard to immigration. They also wanted to move to a country were they would face less of a language barrier. Yet, the global economic downturn of 2008 very negatively influenced the Spanish economy, leading to rising unemployment, which now provides fewer incentives to migrants to move there and makes it harder for immigrants who are already there.[18]

Remittances and other support for family in their countries of origin will continue in the foreseeable future. It is important to remember that these funds play a central economic role in the daily life of many families in the non-Western world. Many immigrants feel responsible for their relatives' well being. They understand the poverty that exists in the places from where they came from. They appreciate how a little bit of money can make a difference in improving the quality of life of their loved ones. Immigrants from various ethnic and racial backgrounds frequently mention and appreciate the opportunities that they have in the United States in terms of work, material well-being, and education.

Thus, they try to give back to relations in their country of origin, and they are willing to make sacrifices for this. To support their families in the United States and abroad many immigrants work multiple jobs in order to put aside more money. They live extremely frugally and try to save on housing, food, and in various other areas.

Marriage

Just as in mainstream American society, marriage is a pillar of immigrant family life. The majority of newcomers marry out of love,

A Vietnamese-American wedding. South Vietnamese and western elements are incorporated into the celebration. David Butow/CORBIS SABA.

while others have arranged marriages, and a few live in polygamous relationships. Furthermore, intermarriage between various ethnic groups has also become a growing social phenomenon that often involves people of immigrant backgrounds.

The majority of immigrants marry for romantic reasons, but in many Middle Eastern, Asian, and African sending societies some marriages are arranged. Even though this does not necessarily comply with American cultural norms and perceptions of what a marriage "should be," this practice is continued among some newcomers. A man who immigrated to the United States from Africa explained the reasons why he gave into an arranged marriage, which was suggested to him by his parents and close relatives.

Knowing the negative perception of this marital arrangement by mainstream society, he was initially a little uncomfortable mentioning this issue. "It was an arranged marriage I should say. She was home and I was here and we corresponded. We initially saw each other in New York, but it wasn't a situation where we dated each other. Some people think that's weird." He explained the rational behind his decision and the tensions surrounding arranged marriages:

I think people consider the family and the impact it will have on the family if things don't work out, so people try to make it work. . . . I think the younger folks have moved away from that. The folks who are educated tend to want to go through this romantic thing first, so it's strange. I am not a traditional person. I think part of it was that I didn't want to disappoint my parents.[19]

It is important to point out that many arranged marriages are happy supporting relationships. The man and his wife have been together for 25 years, and they also have two children together. It is important to remember that any relationship whether arranged or romantic requires the commitment and hard work of the two partners involved.

Even though plural marriages or polygamy, meaning being married to more than one spouse, is not legal in the United States, there are some immigrants who have secretly married multiple spouses. Many of them are Muslims, although mosques in the United States discourage the practice. Academics estimate that there might be some 50,000 to a 100,000 polygamous Muslim families in the United States. It is important to emphasize, however, that not all of these families are of immigrant background or that all polygamists in the United States are Muslims.

Polygamy is not an uncontested issue among adherents to Islam in the United States. There is a vibrant debate on this issue. Proponents of polygamy argue that the precedent for the practice was set by the Prophet Muhammad, who had several wives. The Qu'ran permits a husband to marry as many as four wives. Yet, it also states that the husband should respect and treat all his wives equally. Many Muslims believe that this is impossible. Therefore, polygamy only worked for an exceptional person like Muhammad. Thus, many Muslims, male and female, reject the practice.

There are a variety of issues that influence the opinions of Muslim immigrants on polygamy. According to National Public Radio, "polygamy is more common among conservative, less educated immigrants from Africa and Asia." Some immigrants from these regions want to maintain the tradition of their sending society when they come to the United States. "It is rarer among middle-class Muslims from the Middle East. . . . [N]owadays, imams do background checks on the grooms to make sure they're not already married in their home countries."

"Here's how a man gets around the laws," reports NPR. "He marries one woman under civil law, and then marries one, two, or three others in religious ceremonies that are not recognized by the state. In other cases, men marry women in both America and abroad." Despite the fact that polygamy is illegal in the United States, some clerics are believed to secretly perform weddings.

Women's responses on this issue are complex and diverse. Many Muslim women accept that their husbands have multiple wives for cultural reasons, while others, fearing their husband's or their community's retribution, remain quiet on this issue. Furthermore, in many cases a woman's immigration or asylum status is tied to that of her husband. Thus, they often fear that speaking out on this issue or leaving their partner might get them and their children deported by the federal government or sent back to their sending societies by their husbands.[20]

Intermarriage between people of various "ethnic" and "racial" backgrounds is an interesting sociological phenomenon that has influenced the makeup of many families in recent decades. It is in part also a reason why a growing number of individuals today declare that they are of multiethnic or multiracial background on the Census. Intermarriage will continue to have an altering impact on how Americans perceive and understand their racial and ethnic identity and will continue to change the American mosaic in the future.

Immigrants involved in same-sex relationships face a particularly complicated set of circumstances. Same-sex marriages or civil unions are not federally recognized, and thus do not hold up under federal law. Thus, immigrants as well U.S. citizens who are in a relationship with a foreigner

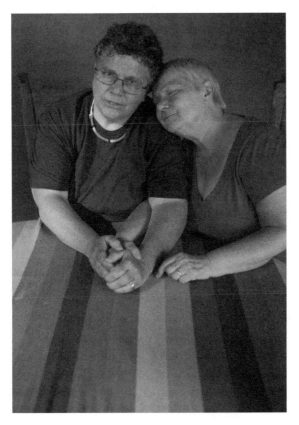

A same-sex couple with one foreign-born person who has no legal status. U.S. law does not allow the citizen in a same-sex couple to sponsor their partner, but permits citizens married to non-citizens in heterosexual relationships to do so. AP Photo/Paul Sakuma.

of the same sex do not have the same rights and opportunities as hetero-sexual couples.

If a same-sex couple wants to marry or commit to a civil union to enable the non-American citizen to stay in the country, for example, this relation-ship will not be recognized by federal immigration authorities even though it might be legal in the state of residence of the couple. Thus, the foreign-born person, unless he or she finds a different way to obtain the required papers, will not be allowed to stay in the country. This legal rea-soning would not be used if the couple comprised a woman and a man.

Challenging Gender Dynamics

Gender dynamics are being challenged in many immigrant households. One reason is that women often not only fulfill their sending society's "traditional" domestic roles as housewives, but they are also part of the workforce. Two incomes are increasingly becoming a necessity for fami-lies to survive. The increased responsibilities and travails between doing housework and working full or part time to contribute money to the fam-ily can lead women to become more assertive in their relationships.

In addition, due to their life in the United States some immigrant women have adopted the cultural, political, and social norms of their host society. This might be another reason for them to be more assertive in a relationship, and it might lead to clashes with the social norms of their sending societies. Some immigrant men can see such developments as a challenge to their authority, which can lead to problems at home between couples.

The Second Generation and the 1.5 Generation

Scholars of immigration generally refer to the children of immigrants who are born in the United States as the "second generation." Their parents are called the "first generation." Children who came to the United States at a young age are sometimes named the "1.5 generation." There are differences and, as we will see in more detail later in the chapter, sometimes tensions emerging between the two generations. Furthermore, people in the second generation are likely to be less versed in their parents' native language, especially in writing.

On the other hand, they are generally more fluent in English and are more likely to speak with an American accent. In 2000, the second gener-ation, which consists of individuals who have at least one foreign-born parent and who were born in America, was estimated to be about 10 per-cent of the overall population. This means that in terms of numbers the second generation is about as strong as the foreign-born population. This underscores once again the tremendous impact that immigration is having on the American mosaic.

Child Rearing

Immigrants, just like mainstream Americans, derive pleasures from but also face challenges when it comes to raising children. In many communities, establishing a family is valued and socially expected. The challenges of raising children are certainly not unique to immigrants, though for various reasons they often face a different set of problems and circumstances. Furthermore, like their American-born counterparts, foreign-born Americans and residents are concerned about finding adequate child care. They worry about their children's education as well as many other issues.

It is frequently the case in several immigrant communities that grandparents carry out many of the childrearing responsibilities. Both parents often work at least one, and in many cases even two or three, jobs. Thus, children go either to daycare or stay with grandparents. There are concerns about the way in which the children and grandchildren of immigrants are intellectually challenged. Many have no access to computers and Internet connections at their grandparents' and often at their parents' houses, putting them at a disadvantaged position to many children in mainstream society.

Especially at a time in history when computer literacy is an increasingly crucial skill needed for career advancement, some children can be left behind in their intellectual development. Furthermore, the limited English abilities of some grandparents and parents can mean that children receive little assistance with their homework and schoolwork. This can put them in a disadvantaged position academically compared to their peers who do not have foreign-born parents or whose parents speak English.

There can be social implications when children have better English skills than their grandparents and parents. Such knowledge of language can provide them with a certain degree of power over their guardians, who rely on their children as translators when they interact with authorities, services, or businesses. In this capacity, the children often serve as translators on school-related issues. This can create problems. It might be in the interest of the student to mistranslate or mischaracterize the severity of a situation they might find themselves in, so that he or she will not to get in trouble with the parents. These issues can play out especially in regard to education.

There is also a transnational component to child rearing. Some immigrants chose to leave behind or send back their children to be raised by family members in their countries of origin. It is not uncommon for children to move back and forth between the United States and their parents' place of birth. Many of these children are citizens of the United States because they were born in America. Others are being left behind by their parents because they have no papers to come to the United States.

"By distributing the task of production and reproduction transnation-
ally," immigrants "create and strengthen their transnational community.
Migrant family members earn most of the household income, while non-
migrants remain behind to care for children. Transnational ties grow stronger
as household members become more and more dependent on one another."
Immigrants often come from societies where the raising of children is a
shared responsibility among multiple family members and where family
boundaries are more fluid. This system continues to be utilized by some
migrants when they leave their sending society for the United States.

Transnational childrearing can pose challenges. Long separation
between parents and children are emotionally difficult, even when there
is access to cheaper communication via phone or airplane travel provides
opportunities to visit. It can stir emotions of loneliness and neglect among
children. Moving between two countries can also be problematic for some
children, as they lack a sense of belonging to either place. This is especially the case if the back-and-forth relocations are relatively frequent
and for extended periods of time. It can lead to disrespectful behavior at
home and at school and to tensions in the family.[21]

Cultural Transmittance and Language Preservation

Transmitting their sending society's culture to their children is important to many immigrants, and this is often done through the family. Food
and family socializing is a main way to keep culture alive. In the minds of
many immigrants, having their children eat the traditional food of home
countries plays a very important role in this process. "For my family," a
Vietnamese American explained, "we are just using food and the family
weekend gatherings. We always eat Vietnamese food on the weekend.
So it continues."[22]

The same man created a Vietnamese language program "because in my
own [extended] family we have some twenty kids." For the father of five
children, the desire for his kids to learn Vietnamese in a formal and struc-
tured way became a priority:

I started the Vietnamese Language Program eleven years ago. Now that program
seems to meet the need of [a] lot of Vietnamese people. We have about 100 students in the program and ten teachers. We run thirty weeks per year starting in
September. Like the school year. . . . The goal of the Vietnamese Family Program
is for the youth to become instructors for the next generation, so that we are able
to carry on that mission. So as soon as they finish the program after eight years . . .
they're invited to become a teaching assistant for two years or three years. Then
they become instructors. Usually they instruct the lower classes. The elders like
myself, we cover the upper classes including the culture poetry, and everything
else. . . . Since I'm a teacher I know how to create curriculum. I am able to work
with the group and create our own curriculum. We are revising it every year.
It is a working model.[23]

Weekend language schools for the children of immigrants can be found all over the United States. They are being taught in cultural centers, clubs, temples, churches, and other places of worship, as well as in regular school buildings. Sometimes when the groups of language learners are smaller, these programs can be run in people's homes.

Often, and quite understandably, the U.S.-born siblings do not have the same linguistic abilities as their foreign-born sibling or their parents. This sometimes can lead to playful teasing, as they make grammatical mistakes or speak with accents. One young Indian American tells about her American-born brother's efforts to learn her native language. "My brother . . . he was born here," she explained. "So it took him a while to get the language down. When he was younger he used to say stuff and people would wonder what he was trying to say. We make fun of him all of the time, but he is picking it up."

At the same time, foreign-born siblings and parents can be quite proud of the achievements of the language learner, and they are often sympathetic about how difficult it is to learn a foreign language in the United States. Nevertheless, this can be an often frustrating and challenging experience.[24]

Most immigrants as well as members of the 1.5 and the second generation want their children to learn their sending society's language. They see this as an important part of their personal and cultural identity. An Indian-American woman explains that she and her friends would want their children "to know the[ir] language." Like many new immigrants, she sees language preservation as an essential part of maintaining traditions. "We want to pass down traditions, basic Indian traditions."[25]

Historically the United States has a reputation for stamping out foreign languages and urging the children of immigrants to use English. Some scholars have referred to America as a "language cemetery." Most researchers believe that it takes about an average of three generations for immigrants to linguistically assimilate. The first generation generally learns some English, but continues to speak their native tongue. The second generation is bilingual. The third generation mostly speaks English.

These generalized trends, many argue, are likely to continue in the future, but for this new wave of immigrants it is too early to be certain. The rules may apply to some ethnic or immigrant groups and minorities while others might be able to potentially maintain their language in the future, especially as continued immigration as well as the relatively easy access to travel and communication might keep the use of foreign languages alive.[26]

Language preservation, many immigrants believe, depends on relatives and the community. One Indian-American woman explains, "I feel like it depends on your family and how you are brought up. If my brother hadn't been brought up this way he wouldn't have spoken [our language], but with my parents and having my sister and me always talk to him, it has helped him." She elaborates on this issue, explaining that her cousins, "the ones that were born here . . . they speak better . . . than I do, but that has to do with their parents." Furthermore, several immigrants emphasize that there needs to be an available infrastructure, like the above-mentioned language programs, to assist families in teaching their loved ones their native tongue.[27]

Intergenerational Issues

The issue of cultural transmission and the maintenance of traditions and traditional identities can also lead to tensions with one's self and within the family. Often this is a generational issue. One Cambodian-American woman explains that when she "was younger, the most important thing for me was to be able to fit in at school and to fit in with my friends. I tried to assimilate and tried to be like them as best as I could. I even sacrificed my own language and my own culture sometimes."

When she grew older, however, she had a change of heart. "Now I realize that my culture and language and my Khmer identity are very important to me, and that I should try to maintain it, and also work with the community to try to preserve it for the young generation as well."[28] Thus, tradition and cultural preservation are often rediscovered by people who had rejected them in their youth to better fit in with their friends in mainstream society. It is also important to underscore that this is not always the case, however, and for many immigrants in the 1.5 and the second generation the rejection remains permanent.

It is vital not to over-exaggerate the intergenerational conflict among immigrants, but also not to see these struggles as something unique to their experience. Immigrant families in the United States certainly have tensions among relatives of different age groups, which are distinct and different from families in mainstream society. Nevertheless, it is important to remember that the search for more independence among adolescents is also a cause of frictions in many "conventional" American families. It is part of the growing-up experience of many teenagers and the parents who raise them.

Intergenerational tensions reflect the complexity and diversity of the immigrant experience and identity formation. The experience of a young Vietnamese-American man in his mid-20s provides a glimpse of these issues:

I've been Americanized a lot. I'm the first one in the family that would break out. The traditional Vietnamese way, I don't really like it that much. I like to try new things. I look at the old way, but I also want to see what is out there. So a lot of traditional rules I do not follow, or refuse to follow. . . . There are tensions, but there's nothing my parents can do, because I'm a grown up.

At the same time, many among the younger generation still maintain their culture and try to walk a path between two worlds. The same Vietnamese

American explains, "How do I maintain my cultural identity? Usually what I do is celebrate the [Vietnamese] New Year. I promote my culture by doing a traditional performance, like an opera, and musical performances. . . . I also bought a Vietnamese Zither. I learned how to play the zither on my own."[29] The comments by a young Cambodian-American woman reflect these views. "Our culture and our traditions . . . it is so intertwined. . . . Even though I'm really Americanized, and a modern-day . . . young adult, but I do follow the tradition and culture . . . it's important."[30]

Complaints among some older immigrants about the younger generation are based on what is often perceived as "lack of respect" and "unruliness." Some feel that the youth is being changed by mainstream society in a way that has disrupted a more traditional order. One older man who came to the United States as a refugee from Laos explained:

I think the school system here, from kindergarten to twelve, if they taught what they teach in our country, how to be men, how to respect, not to do bad things . . . we would call them family values, right? Teach religion in school. . . . There is too much freedom . . . students talk back at teachers . . . not in our country. . . . Their life here is different. Right now I can't even talk to my grandchildren. Whatever your parent and grandparents say to you are supposed to say, "Yes grandmother, yes grandfather." Here they say, "I can't do it, I don't want to do it, I hate you." Now this is totally wrong. And it shocked me. I cannot depend on them. In our country when you get old you can depend on your children to take care of you. Here, forget it![31]

Two sociologists write that "intergenerational conflicts may be particularly acute in groups whose cultural patterns and practices differ radically from those in the broader American culture. In this regard, it is important to note that immigrant parents" as well as grandparents "often hold up an idealized version of traditional values and customs as a model for their children, even though these values and customs have often undergone considerable change since immigrants left the home country." These reinventions of the past might serve to legitimate and strengthen the authority of parents and grandparents within the family.[32]

The younger age group, who were either born in the United States or who arrived here early during their childhood, grew up exposed to American culture, with its emphasis on independence and individualism. The sociological changes that this exposure can cause are certainly not lost on the younger generation. An Indian-American woman in her early twenties explains that she sometimes communicates with her parents about this issue. "In India it's more like you're just dependent on your parents. Everybody here is like, 'I need to get a job,' or 'I get to have a job' . . . but in India you solely focus on school and then after school you go on to work . . . but until then you're basically dependent on your parents."

Her friend added that that was "one major difference I found too . . . you learn to take care of yourself at an early age . . . in India everyone depends on their parents. You wouldn't want to be by yourself. You wouldn't want to get a job."[33] Thus, independence and individualism come with a completely different set of responsibilities and challenges for the 1.5 and the second generation.

The drive for independence, responsibility, and outspokenness by some among the younger generation can also on occasion lead to conflict with older immigrants, who are, at times, perceived as controlling and authoritarian. Many younger people feel, however, that authority and respect is something to be earned. A young Cambodian-American community activist expresses her feelings on this issue. "Just because you're older than me you demand respect? My mom always gets mad at me when I talk bad about somebody who is older. But I just don't believe in the things that they've done for the community. So I'd be talking back to them, and she's like, 'How could you? They're older than you?' And 'Don't ruin our family name.' "[34]

Furthermore, intergenerational issues can play themselves out with regard to going out at night, the way people dress, music, decorating one's room, dance, dating, sexual relations, and marriage beyond an ethnic group.

Sometimes members of the 1.5 and the second generation clash with their relatives over the issue of arranged marriage. Influenced by mainstream culture, many in the younger age group desire to marry out of love or for romantic reasons, and they resist their parents' efforts to set them up with someone they do not know and have no relationship with. Other children, out of what they see as respect and love for their elders, go along with their parents' or other relatives' wishes, at least to a degree.

This, however, can at times lead to feelings of cultural disconnection— meaning that individuals feel trapped between two cultures, the one of the sending country and that of the United Sates. This has also led to the growing presence of what scholars refer to as semi-arranged marriages, which leave young immigrants with more choices and veto power in the decision process of who to marry. This arrangement works for some, but is rejected by many others who do not want to engage in certain cultural practices of their parents.

Another frequent point of intergenerational tensions involves the expectations by immigrant parents for their children to do well. This relates generally to the children's performance in school. Some parents feel that they gave up a lot to get their families to the United States, and now they expect strong academic performance from their kids to make their sacrifice worthwhile. In many sending societies there is also a cultural expectation that children will take care of their parents in old age. This leads some parents to push their children toward careers that they believe will be financially rewarding and secure.

Such pressures can occasionally alienate the children of immigrants, who can feel that too much responsibility and too high of expectations are put on their shoulders. Instead, they would like to follow their dreams and pursue a career in which they are truly interested. Still, it is important to point out that in many cases the young generation pursues its goals and, despite a period of tension at times, continues to maintain positive relations with its parents.[35]

Furthermore, many in the 1.5 generation and the second generation are also very driven students, eager to improve their life and future through education. "We push ourselves," two Indian-American college students who immigrated to the United States, one at age six, the other in her early teens, explain. Peer pressure can sometimes be as enticing to perform well as parental expectations. One of them explains, "When I was in India, I remember as a kid I didn't want to go to school, but my cousins pushed me more . . . this is the way I was brought up and so now I push myself."[36]

NOTES

1. Stephen Castles and Mark Miller, *The Age of Migration: International Population Movements in the Modern World*, Third Edition (New York: The Guilford Press, 2003).

2. Peggy Levitt, *The Transnational Villagers* (Berkeley, MA: University of California Press, 2001), 3–5.

3. Emile Tabea interviewed by Christoph Strobel, January 16, 2008, Ethnographic Study of Lowell, MA.

4. Bryan Tran interviewed by Christoph Strobel, Craig Thomas, and Yingchan Zhang, May 8, 2008, Ethnographic Study of Lowell, MA.

5. Anonymous 1 (Indian) and Anonymous 2 (Indian) interviewed by Christoph Strobel, December 14, 2007, Ethnographic Study of Lowell, MA.

6. Lisa Dagdigian interviewed by Christoph Strobel, March 28, 2008, Ethnographic Study of Lowell, MA.

7. Ana Suarez interviewed by Christoph Strobel, Craig Thomas, and Yingchan Zhang, February 29, 2008, Ethnographic Study of Lowell, MA.

8. Tony Mai interviewed by Christoph Strobel, April 25, 2008, Ethnographic Study of Lowell, MA.

9. Sidney Liang interviewed by Christoph Strobel, January 17, 2009, Ethnographic Study of Lowell, MA.

10. Sidney Liang interviewed by Christoph Strobel, January 17, 2009, Ethnographic Study of Lowell, MA.

11. Bryan Tran interviewed by Christoph Strobel, Craig Thomas, and Yingchan Zhang, May 8, 2008, Ethnographic Study of Lowell, MA.

12. Anonymous 6 (Polish) interviewed by Christoph Strobel and Yingchan Zhang, May 2, 2008, Ethnographic Study of Lowell, MA.

13. Emile Tabea interviewed by Christoph Strobel, January 16, 2008, Ethnographic Study of Lowell, MA.

14. Emile Tabea interviewed by Christoph Strobel, January 16, 2008, Ethnographic Study of Lowell, MA.

15. James Painter, "US Woes Slow Migrant Remittances," March 12, 2008, *BBC News*. http://news.bbc.co.uk/go/pr/fr/-/2//hi/americas/7292216.stm (accessed April 28, 2008).

16. Levitt, *The Transnational Villagers*, 73.

17. Painter, "US Woes Slow Migrant Remittances," "Remittances to Mexico: The End of the American Dream," *The Economist*, December 13, 2008, 46; "U.S. Mexicans Send Less Money Home," October 1, 2008, *BBC News*. http://news.bbc.co.uk/go/pr/fr/-/2/hi/business/7647132.stm (accessed October 3, 2008).

18. Painter, "US Woes Slow Migrant Remittances," "Remittances to Mexico," 46; "U.S. Mexicans Send Less Money Home."

19. Bowa Tucker interviewed by Christoph Strobel, January 6, 2008, Ethnographic Study of Lowell, MA.

20. Barbara Bradley Hagerty, "Some Muslims in U.S. Quietly Engage in Polygamy," aired on *All Things Considered*, National Public Radio, May 27, 2008. http://www.npr.org/templates/story/story.php?storyId=90857818&sc=emaf (accessed May 28, 2008).

21. Levitt, *The Transnational Villagers*, 75.

22. Thong Phamduy interviewed by Christoph Strobel, April 30, 2008, Ethnographic Study of Lowell, MA.

23. Thong Phamduy interviewed by Christoph Strobel, April 30, 2008, Ethnographic Study of Lowell, MA.

24. Anonymous 1 (Indian) and Anonymous 2 (Indian) interviewed by Christoph Strobel, December 14, 2007, Ethnographic Study of Lowell, MA.

25. Anonymous 1 (Indian) and Anonymous 2 (Indian) interviewed by Christoph Strobel, December 14, 2007, Ethnographic Study of Lowell, MA.

26. David Lopez and Vanesa Estrada, "Language," in *The New Americans: A Guide to Immigration Since 1965*, ed. Mary Waters and Reed Ueda (Cambridge, MA: Harvard University Press, 2007), 230.

27. Anonymous 1 (Indian) and Anonymous 2 (Indian) interviewed by Christoph Strobel, December 14, 2007, Ethnographic Study of Lowell, MA.

28. Phala Chea interviewed by Christoph Strobel, January 15, 2008, Ethnographic Study of Lowell, MA.

29. Bryan Tran interviewed by Christoph Strobel, Craig Thomas, and Yingchan Zhang, May 8, 2008, Ethnographic Study of Lowell, MA.

30. Sambath Bo interviewed by Christoph Strobel, April 15, 2008, Ethnographic Study of Lowell, MA.

31. Blong Xiong interviewed by Christoph Strobel, March 15, 2008, Ethnographic Study of Lowell, MA.

32. Nancy Foner and Philip Kasinitz, "The Second Generation," in *The New Americans*, 276–277.

33. Anonymous 1 (Indian) and Anonymous 2 (Indian) interviewed by Christoph Strobel, December 14, 2007, Ethnographic Study of Lowell, MA.

34. Sambath Bo interviewed by Christoph Strobel, April 15, 2008, Ethnographic Study of Lowell, MA.

35. Foner and Kasinitz, 278–279.

36. Anonymous 1 (Indian) and Anonymous 2 (Indian) interviewed by Christoph Strobel, December 14, 2007, Ethnographic Study of Lowell, MA.

4

COMMUNITY, MAINSTREAM SOCIETY, AND CULTURE

Many immigrants in the United States have embraced and grown comfortable in the cities, towns, villages, and rural areas where they live. The processes of turning a host community into a permanent home community, however, are developments that happen on many complex and diverse levels. In previous chapters we have already discussed how some immigrants create businesses that cater to the particular tastes and interests of their specific ethnic groups.

These developments aid in the creation of places in which the newcomers feel comfortable, sometimes at a level that a whole area becomes an "ethnic neighborhood." Furthermore, religious, social, and cultural institutions, as well as the celebration of festivals and holidays, also feature very centrally in these developments and aid in the creation and maintenance of immigrant communities and identities.

Immigrant daily life is also influenced by the interactions with American mainstream society into which the newcomers are integrated to various degrees. As discussed in Chapter 2, many immigrants are part of the economy as laborers, entrepreneurs, and consumers. However, interaction with mainstream American society happens not only on an economic level. For instance, the children of immigrants and members of the 1.5 generation make up a growing percentage of the country's student body. Furthermore, the newcomers also interact with the social, the health care, and the criminal justice system.

The intersection of immigrant community and mainstream society also has an impact on immigrant culture. As new identities are being formed through their daily life in the United States, immigrants create and consume fashion, music, and dance, which often mix elements of their sending society with aspects of American culture.

RELIGION AND RELIGIOUS INSTITUTIONS

Due to the tremendous diversity among immigrants who came to the United States since 1965, the country's religious landscape has been tremendously enriched by people from virtually all corners of the globe. Today, believers of all major world religions live in the United States.

Immigrants do not only bring their economic, political, and social aspirations with them, but also their belief systems, scriptures, customs, and traditions. Immigrants are building their places of worship all over the country. For many, attending a church, temple, mosque, or a synagogue is generally the most common way in which they participate in community life. Communities of faith play an important role in the daily life of many immigrants, just as they figure prominently in the life of many Americans in mainstream society. This section of the chapter briefly discusses some of the major religions and religious institutions, but it provides by no means a complete picture of the diverse and complex religious landscape among immigrants.

It is important to underscore that even within immigrant communities of faiths there exists tremendous diversity, which is often due to regional and sectarian differences that exist among major world religions. In addition, in many instances the newcomers move alongside co-religionists who have arrived in the United States before 1965 or who are mainstream American converts.

While religion plays an important role in the daily life of many immigrants, it is important to remember that, just as in mainstream American society, not everyone identifies as being religious or regularly attends services in places of worship. Thus, while religion and religious institutions influence the daily life of many newcomers, others cherish the right not to be tied to a religious tradition.[1]

Hinduism

There is tremendous diversity among immigrants in the United States who identify as Hindu. The religion varies along regional, caste, class, and sectarian lines. It is a complex and varied collection of beliefs, many of which are based on scriptures called the Veda and the teachings of the Upanishads. Many practices are also linked to regions or are caste specific. The incredible diversity of beliefs and practices is evident in Hindu communities across the United States. There are an estimated 1.3 million Hindus living in America. Many of the immigrants of Hindu faith come from India, but some are also part of the Indian global diaspora of the nineteenth and twentieth century, originating, for example, from East Africa, the Caribbean, or Great Britain. Furthermore, there are also an estimated 250,000 Sikhs and about 20,000 Jains, two religious communities that also originated in India and who are now living in the United States.[2]

Temples play a central role in the religious life of Hindus. Similar to Christian churches, which generally are built along a cross-like outline, Hindu temples in India and elsewhere around the world are often constructed around a pattern of a human-shaped figure enclosed by a square. This is of course the idealized architectural design of a temple. Just as churches today are often laid out in different ways, however, many temples, rather than being constructed from scratch, are being put into existing structures such as industrial parks and therefore do not fulfill the established ideals of the past.

Nevertheless, the places of worship still fulfill the spiritual needs of temple attendees. Temples have sacred images generally of the Hindu deities, such as Vishnu or Shiva, to which the temple is dedicated, and services can take place several times a day. Furthermore, the temples are usually open during the day for attendees so that they can come in to perform their religious prayers and practices.[3]

Buddhism

Buddhism is a major religion among many Asians in the United States. As with Hinduism there are quite diverse beliefs among practicing Buddhists. These differences often depend on people's regional origins and the specific sect of Buddhism they belong to. There are an estimated 3 million to 4 million Buddhists living in the United States, many of which are immigrants.

There are various Buddhist temples throughout the United States that serve as places of worship but also as centers for immigrant communities to meet. A Lao Buddhist temple in Lowell, Massachusetts, is representative of many Buddhist temples used by Asian immigrants. This place of worship can be found in a quiet residential neighborhood. In this particular temple the monks reside in a building to the left of the main entrance. On the right is the main temple hall, which was built a few years ago. The temple is painted in yellow with red and green designs decorating the eaves. As you enter the temple you remove your shoes.

The main temple has a kitchen area in which women prepare food for the monks and at times also for the members of the community who visit the temple during festivals and holy days. This is often a place where women socialize and catch up. As one enters the main hall of the temple you can see the statue of a golden Buddha sitting on an altar. The hall is encircled with paintings depicting aspects of the life story of the Buddha. During festivals and holy days the temple facilities are packed with visitors and worshippers.

Islam

According to one demographic study conducted in 2000, there are an estimated 1,400 mosques in the United States. The researchers believed that the active religious membership of these institutions was at about 2 million. The same team of researchers estimated that there were about 6 million to 7 million Muslims living in the United States. This number includes African Americans who are believed to make up about 30 percent of the Muslim population. Other estimates put the number of Muslims in the United States at 2.8 million and at 4.1 million.[4]

There is not only diversity among Muslims due to the fact that some are American and others are foreign born, but also because Muslim immigrants come from all corners of the Islamic world. Thus, there are dramatic cultural and religious differences. The largest portion of Muslim immigrants to the United States comes from South Asia, such as Pakistan, Bangladesh, and India, as well as from the Arab world, reaching all across the Middle East. However, Muslim immigrants also come from countries in western Africa like Senegal or the Gambia as well as from places in Southeast Asia, such as Thailand or Indonesia.

The United States has also become the home for Muslim refugees of war, who come from diverse places such as Somalia in East Africa or Bosnia in the Balkan region of Eastern Europe. Thus, depending on the diversity and volume of immigrants in certain areas, Islamic community centers and mosques can cater to an exclusive ethnic clientele such as South Asian Urdu speakers, while others can serve a much more diverse audience, recruiting their membership and worshippers from a wider ethnic and national base.[5]

Judaism

Judaism alongside Islam and Christianity is one of the three major monotheistic religions in the United States. Synagogues and Jewish religious communities are well established. While there have been Jewish families in America since independence, many Jewish immigrants came to the country in the late nineteenth and early twentieth century, especially from Eastern Europe, where many fled poverty and religious persecution. In more recent years, most Jewish immigrants have come to the United States from the former Soviet Union and from the state of Israel.

The Jewish community life centers around the synagogue, which traditionally has an ark or cupboard on the wall that faces towards Jerusalem. This is where the community keeps the scrolls of Pentateuch, the first five books of the Bible and the spiritual centerpiece of Jewish scripture. Central to the synagogue is the *bimah*, generally a raised platform with a reading table where the Pentateuch is read and from where the Cantor leads the prayer in many synagogues. While in many synagogues the sexes sit together, in Orthodox congregations men and women sit separately from one another. Furthermore, and just like in other immigrant places of worship, synagogues and Jewish centers play important roles in their believers' daily life as places where the community can socialize and maintain and develop their cultural identity.

Christianity

Immigration has also enriched the Christian landscape of the United States. There are a variety of new Christian communities emerging throughout the country, such as Latino Catholic as well as Pentecostal and other Protestant churches and African or Korean Presbyterian churches, just to name a few. Furthermore, throughout the nation well-established mainstream places of worship have also been joined by diverse groups of immigrants from Latin America, Asia, and Africa. Many mainline churches have embraced this cultural diversity and cater to the needs of their new membership. There are numerous churches throughout the United States that offer services in English, Spanish, as well as many other languages.

The majority of immigrants with a Christian background are Latino. Since the Latino population has grown from 22.4 million to about 37 million from 1990 to 2003, largely due to immigration, Latinos have also become the largest minority in the United States. These numerical increases have implications for the future. One scholar observes that the "National Conference of Catholic Bishops estimates that by 2050 more than half of all American Catholics will be Latino, and the need for Spanish-speaking priests who understand the devotional vibrancy of Hispanic Catholicism is urgent." Among those Latinos who identify themselves as Christian, an estimated 7 out of 10 are Catholic, and about one out of four is Protestant.

As this numbers makes clear, Latinos are also having an impact on the Protestant landscape in the United States. Latinos, for example, are believed to make up more than 60 percent of the increase in the membership of Assemblies of God churches. Furthermore, "major Protestant denominations, such as the United Methodist Church and the Presbyterian Church USA, have developed active Hispanic/Latino caucuses that bring the new perspectives of immigrants' cultures to the issues and arguments of the denomination." Even among immigrants from the Middle East, Africa, and Asia, immigrants of Christian background have been disproportionately represented in comparison with non-Christians.[6]

Religion and Tensions

Religion not only plays a role in cultural preservation and community building, but it can also reinforce differences, tensions, and divisions among believers and communities. Conflict over religious issues, often deeply imbedded in personal and political tensions, has occurred throughout American history in immigrant communities. It is likely to continue to do so in the future.

The Trairatanaram Temple and Parsonage in North Chelmsford, Massachusetts has been the staging ground for a recent episode that underscores these national trends and observations on a local level. A conflict between monks there, which went to court in 2004, has had a spillover effect into the Cambodian population in the region. Many have chosen sides in this dispute. After threats of violence in the temple community, a court ordered the two factions of monks to separate into the upstairs and the downstairs portion of the temple. This division has led some members in the Cambodian community to call the institution the "Upstairs Downstairs" temple in jest.

There are debates among the monks about who should hold power, who owns the temple, whether leadership should be centralized or decentralized, and how the temple should be engaged with the community. Personality conflicts among the monks further complicate the picture. In addition, there are charges of misappropriation of funds and improper recordkeeping. The dispute has antagonized some members of the Cambodian community in the region. Many in the community have lost their faith in the monks and argue that they have lost all claims to morality because they are tainted by a desire for power that has corrupted them.[7]

At times tensions over religion can be intergenerational. A young Vietnamese man whose family belonged to the Catholic minority in Vietnam and who had immigrated to the United States at a young age explains:

My parent's generation, they are very religious. But for our generation . . . our view of religion and the old Catholic way . . . we want to change with the times a little bit, because some of the rules that they put out, that they try to teach the kids, I think it's just way too strict, or just narrow minded. . . . For my generation, I think that religiously we are not as strict. Yet, I don't know, when I become a parent I don't know how my views are going to change.[8]

Intergenerational disputes about how to live one's life, over attending religious services, as well as over scriptural and spiritual interpretation, can emerge in many immigrant religious communities.

HOLIDAYS

Keeping with their religious beliefs and cultural traditions, many immigrants continue to celebrate their holidays after they come to the United States. These celebrations remind newcomers of the customs of their sending societies and aid in the maintenance of their cultures. Yet, immigrants also change and adapt their holidays to fit their new circumstances, such as by shortening their holidays due to economic and other scheduling realities. Furthermore, many also embrace mainstream American holidays.

Hindu Holidays

Hindus celebrate a number of sacred feasts and holidays. Reflecting Hinduism's tremendous diversity and complexity, religious scholars estimate that there are over 1,000 of them, which are celebrated in various regions and among various Hindu sects and groups. The holidays are based on the lunar cycle, and thus their dates fluctuate in the Western calendar. Some of the major celebrations—but certainly not an exclusive list of them and in no particular order of ranking—are Divali (the festival of lights), Krishnajayanti (commemorating the birth of Krishna), and Holi (the Hindu New Year).

It is also important to underscore that the celebrations of even the major festivals have some regional and sectarian variations. Thus, a Divali celebration at a South Indian temple would have very different elements from that of a temple from a region further to the north, such as a Swaminaryan temple frequented by people from the Gujarat region of India.

Buddhist New Year Celebrations

Among many immigrants from East and Southeast Asia, traditional New Year holidays play an important role. For instance, the Chinese New Year is celebrated by many Chinese immigrants and Chinese Americans. The coming of the new year and the expelling of the old is signified by the cleaning, and traditionally also often the repainting, of the home. Often offerings in the form of sweet rice and wine are given to the god of the stove. Among various other ceremonies affiliated with the Chinese New Year, household gods and the ancestors are being honored by burning candles and incense, as well as by giving food, spirit money, and bows.

Many Southeast Asians spend some time at Buddhist temples during their New Year celebrations. However, celebrating the new year is much more than a religious event. It is very much a family and community affair, a precious time to connect with loved ones, eat good food, enjoy each other's company, and call relatives in Southeast Asian sending societies to catch up and to send best wishes.

Many Southeast Asians who have converted to Christianity continue to celebrate the traditional New Year within the structure of their church. An interviewee describes the Vietnamese New Year's celebration at his Catholic church:

Traditionally we have three days to celebrate, but over here, we don't have that much time . . . we only celebrate one day every year. Here at the church, we have a big feast. Everybody just brings their food and we all share. Hundreds show up for that night at church. Usually we have a pretty big mass. I'm in the church choir and we prepare to sing special songs and we practice for that. And then we also do a talent show. . . . I did a Judo presentation with my sister once . . . we did a traditional opera . . . [ate] a lot of food . . . [and held a] fashion show.[9]

The mixing of culture and processes of cultural syncretism, in part already stemming from French colonization in Vietnam, in part a result of the immigrant experience in the United States, are apparent in this quote and are representative of the processes that many immigrants are undergoing.

Muslim Holidays

American Muslims, whether established in this country for several generations or fairly recent arrivals, celebrate two major holidays. The first one is Eid al-Fitr, which is celebrated after Ramadan, a month of fasting for Muslims. The day generally begins with worship by the congregational community and a sermon by the imam, either in a masjid (mosque), an Islamic Center, or, if larger crowds are expected or if several masjid gather in combined worship and prayer, at a convention center. The rest of the holiday is spent with family and friends, visiting, feasting, and giving gifts for the children.

The other major holiday, the celebration of Eid al-Adha, takes place toward the end of the Hajj. The Hajj is the yearly pilgrimage to Mecca, the place of origin of Islam, which an able-bodied Muslim who has the financial means should do once in his or her lifetime. By observing this holiday, Muslims around the world believe that they participate in the spirit of the Hajj.

The Changing Christian Holiday Calendar

Immigration has also had an impact on the Christian holiday calendar. As mentioned before, the majority of Christian immigrants are Latino. The growing Latino population is especially changing the Catholic Church. Besides having Spanish masses, many Catholic churches have incorporated Latino religious festivals and holidays such as the Day of the Dead or the Day of Our Lady of Guadalupe. Many Catholic churches have also incorporated the Hispanic *posada* processions during advent into their liturgical calendar.

Mainstream American Holidays

Furthermore, a lot of immigrants have also adopted and embraced mainstream American holidays that do not necessarily fit with their religious traditions. One immigrant of Buddhist background explains this national trend:

I celebrate everything ... because celebration is celebration. You don't need to practice specifically your own religion or tradition. You do things that make you happy. Celebrate Christmas? Sure, that makes my family happy. And we celebrate Thanksgiving ... because we value the opportunity to spend time with our family.[10]

Furthermore, some immigrants who are not Christian have taken up some of the traditions loosely related with the Christian Easter holiday, such as organizing Easter egg hunts for their children.

Numerous immigrants observe holidays like Independence Day on the fourth of July, Veteran's Day, Mother's Day, Father's Day, and Memorial Day. For those who served or have family members that have served or currently serve in the United States armed forces, these civil holidays are imbued with special meaning. Family-centered holidays like Father's Day or Mother's Day are also popular among many.

Furthermore, and as the quote above makes clear, numerous immigrants also celebrate a traditional American style Thanksgiving, with the traditional turkey, mashed potatoes, and pie. Others, especially immigrant children, like to "trick or treat," to go to haunted houses, or to partake in numerous other activities during the Halloween holiday.

FESTIVALS

Many immigrants organize festivals as a celebration of their culture and homelands. Such events aid in the formation and definition of group networks and identity. Numerous of these events began as "organic" celebrations, meaning that the groups that stage them often saw an important need for their communities and families to have this celebration as a means of cultural preservation. After some time, however, festivals often transform into events that reflect the agendas of community leaders, who believe that staging such a happening might give their group some wider positive exposure and larger cohesion.[11] One can find a rich variety of immigrant festivals throughout the United States, such as the San Gennaro Italian Festival or the Puerto Rican Parade in New York City, the Chinese New Year in San Francisco, or the "Calle 8" Festival of Miami.

Latino festivals are celebrated all over the country. Sometimes these events have a church connection and are accompanied by a Mass. Many festivals have elaborate processions, with people marching, floats, cars, and flags. A significant part of the festivities are accompanied by food, music, dance, raffles, and games and people wearing dress that represent a wide variety of Latin-American countries.

Puerto Rican street parade in New York City. Mario Tama/Getty Images.

The Latino Festival in Washington, D.C. is an event that helps build community among people from a rich variety of national, ethnic, and racial backgrounds, a diversity that can be observed during the celebration. There are performances by bands that play major Latin-American music styles, such as salsa, merengue, and cumbia, as well as more "traditional" or "folkloric" music and dances, such as ballenata music from Colombia, Mexican mariachi, flamenco, or Andean music.

Many festivals also have stalls that are being used for economic, social, and advocacy purposes. Vendors offer a wide variety of goods, such as ethnic foods, as well as regional products such as crafts, religious and national icons, or flags. At times these sellers can be commercial small business entities trying to make a profit or to increase their profile. At other times they can be church groups or nonprofits, which are selling products such as food or other goods to raise revenue for their organizations. Social services, community groups, unions, and environmental groups often also man stalls or floats at such events to raise awareness of their causes and to do outreach.[12]

The highlight of many festivals is the parade. An observer describes the following scene:

With spectacular decorations and costumes, vibrant rhythms, and flowing choreographies, floats and marchers proceeded.... Paraders created floats by decorating cars, pick up trucks, stake trucks, or flatbed trailers. Marchers included flag bearers, banner carriers, dramatic troupes, bands, clowns, and *camparsas* (carnival troupes with music and dance).[13]

The beautifully ornamented and decorated floats can display anything ranging from flags, national emblems, national political figures and heroes, agricultural and regional products, scenes of daily life, architectural reproductions, labor processes, political and social messages, as well as anything else that the float designers can create.

The Southeast Asian Water Festival in Lowell, Massachusetts also aims to celebrate, maintain, and share Southeast Asian identity and culture. The event attracts about 60,000 people every year. Many Cambodians, Lao, and Vietnamese come to Lowell from across the country for this event. The festival is based on Buddhist traditions, held "to thank the spirit of the water, to pray for evil spirits to go away, and to honor the Dragon King who dwells in the water. The Water Festival is a time to be thankful for the rivers, lakes, and ponds."[14]

In Lowell, the Water Festival happens on the banks of the Merrimack River. One of the festival's highlights are the boat races that occur throughout the day, and in which teams with crews of about 18 to 24 rowers compete in traditional Southeast Asian boats over a stretch of 1,000 meters. There is also a wealth of traditional Southeast Asian dance performances as well as traditional musical performances. But at times the dancers also mix in American cultural elements into their routines, such as hip hop and break dance, to lighten up the mood. Teenagers and young adults perform rap music, which are often performed in Southeast Asian languages such as Khmer. Beauty pageants also play a popular role during the Water Festival. Furthermore, there are many booths where vendors sell a rich variety of Southeast Asian foods, crafts, and traditional clothing.

Events like the Latino Festival or the Southeast Asian Water Festival help in the construction of identity. They help immigrants in the process of self-definition of who they are as individuals but also as a community. The two events help in forging ethnic unity among diverse immigrant groups. Both terms—"Latino" and "Southeast Asian"—are self-embraced and constructed. Both groups include people from diverse and complex national, ethnic, racial, and class backgrounds.

The festival helps "Latino" and "Southeast Asians" to assert that they have a distinct collective identity away from mainstream American society. At the same time, such festivals also celebrate the diversity and difference of the American mosaic, in a sense embracing the United States by inviting the larger public to join in the festivities.[15]

ORGANIZATIONS AND ASSOCIATIONS

With the wave of newcomers who have arrived since the 1960s, there has also been a proliferation of organizations and associations that advocate for the rights of immigrants. These groups can represent specific communities. Organizations that are active on behalf of newcomers can also have pan-immigrant goals, however, meaning that they represent the interests of several ethnic communities or that they are issue-driven organizations, which serve the specific needs of newcomers.

By consolidating interests, by advocating in more general terms, or by focusing on specific issues, these organizations hope to become more effective. They are active in the fields of politics and economics, they pursue cultural goals and ideals, and they advocate on women, family, gender, youth, and educational issues. They attempt to serve the political, economic, cultural, and social needs, and they are often created by immigrants themselves. Thus, they try to play an active and proactive role in the daily life of newcomers.

The evolution of South Asian Organizations in the metropolitan New York City area, which we examine here in more detail, provides a case study that underscores this process on a national level. New York City has seen a proliferation of Indian and South Asian organizations since the 1960s. These associations are serving and addressing countless interests. There is a multi-polarity, complexity, and diversity regarding the Indian community, which is reflected in the diversity of organizations that represent their interests.[16]

South Asian and Indian organizations pursue a variety of goals in the United States. A group called the Association of Indians in America (AIA), for example, is an organization that was founded by Indian professionals in 1967. The group at the time drew support from people that came from a variety of regions on the Indian subcontinent. It united individuals from such diverse regions as Gujarat in western India, Tamil Nadu in southern India, or Orissa in eastern India, just to mention a few areas, each with very distinct social, cultural, and linguistic characteristics.

It would have been unlikely that Indians of such diverse backgrounds would present such a united front on such a large scale in 1960s India. In the United States, however, pan-Indian organizations like the AIA pursued unified strategies, realizing that they would be politically more effective. Being in the United States aided in the creation of a pan-Indian identity among people from the subcontinent, who realized that there was much more that united them than divided them.

The AIA worked and is working on issues regarding "the social welfare of the Asian Indians in the United States, and to help them become a part of the mainstream of American life." In the 1970s, for example, the association "lobbied the Commerce Department for an 'Asian Indian' choice in the U.S. Census under the 'Asian Pacific Islander' category." In the 1970s as well, the AIA successfully lobbied for the extension of "Minority Status to the immigrants of South Asian Americans for civil rights purposes."[17]

While the AIA and other organizations like it clearly advocate for the rights of Indian Americans and South Asian Americans, they also remain active on an international level. For example, the AIA raised money during the tsunami catastrophe in 2004. This natural disaster had a devastating impact on many countries in South and Southeast Asia. Many immigrant communities in the United States with members who originated from this part of the world launched relief efforts in their sending societies to deal with the disaster. Furthermore such organizations also support such causes as the fight against HIV and AIDS as well as developmental programs.[18]

Women and youth associations also figure prominently among the South Asians in New York City. Starting in the 1980s several women's organizations emerged that began to focus on gender issues. Among these groups was Asian Indian Women in America (AIWA), Manawi, and Sakhi. AIWA was ideologically and sociologically closest to the AIA. It recruited its constituency among upper- and upper-middle-class women. AIWA helped women to network professionally. It held job fairs and advocated against racial discrimination against Indian women professionals. Its outreach to Indian immigrant women from lower economic and educational backgrounds was much more limited, however. Organizations like Manawi and Sakhi developed much more effective strategies to reach out to women from these social classes. They also run programs to deal with domestic violence, operate emergency shelters, and offer programs to deal with sexual harassment, assault, and rape.[19]

Several incidents of anti-Indian and anti-South Asian violence in the mid-1980s spurred a wave of youth activism and the creation of youth organizations, developments that occurred in similar ways in other parts of the United States in various immigrant communities. The assaults in the greater New York City area reminded younger South Asians of their status as a racial minority in America and spurred them to create a number of anti-racist organizations. Young South-Asian Americans also created associations that advocated for Lesbian and Gay rights and for AIDS awareness.

Although these groups addressed dissimilar issues, they all had similar characteristics. One observer writes that "[b]ecause their members had grown up either in the United States with a sense of racial consciousness or in the South Asian progressive world, themes of racial and ethnic discrimination, social justice, and equality were integral to their agendas."[20]

Furthermore, and despite the fact that South Asia is a region with turbulent relations between neighboring countries such as Pakistan and India, many young South Asians in the United States have learned to find more that unites than divides them. Their taste in music, film, and food, for example, often overlap, and they frequently feel that they face similar challenges and forms of discrimination from mainstream American society. Many feel comfortable in embracing a pan-regional identity as South-Asian Americans alongside—and sometimes rather than—an Indian or Pakistani American identity.[21]

Still, many South-Asian cultural associations have a strong regional rather than a pan-Indian focus. While most Indians and Indian-born immigrants acknowledge and are proud of their national identity, many also argue that their regional traditions and languages are equally important. Thus, cultural organizations in the United States are often built around the regional identity of Indian states such as Gujarat, Bengal, or Bihar, as well as around "ethnic" groups that believe themselves to have distinct identities.

It is important to keep in mind that the regional states that make up India have populations as large, or larger, than many of the world's sovereign nation-states. India, after all, is a country whose population today is estimated to be more than 1 billion people.[22]

There is a tremendous abundance and diversity of cultural associations in the United States. They pursue a wide variety of goals, including the preservation, heritage, and celebration of distinct regional and national languages, cultures, history, traditions, festivals, dance, and foods. They are popular with many immigrants who see them as an important part of their daily life in the United States, since these groups often provide community and a connection to a previous life.

Some immigrant cultural organizations offer classes for young immigrants and the children of immigrants, where the youth can learn the language of their family's sending society. The classes generally meet on weekends and after school and enable the next generation to carry on their family's cultural heritage in a new land. These languages are also often spoken at home.

There are also organizations that celebrate dance and music. Immigrant dance groups commemorate and preserve traditional and classical dances from their native countries, but they also teach these skills to a new generation. Others safeguard and honor the music of their country of origin. They practice, study, and perform their native classical and traditional instruments, compositions, and songs, and teach their trade to the younger age groups.

Other cultural associations combine the performance of dance and music. These dance and music groups play at religious and cultural institutions, at family celebrations such as weddings and festivals, at events that celebrate the ethnic heritage of an immigrant community, and at many other venues.

It is important to reiterate, however, that cultures are not static phenomenon. They are fluid, and they change. This can certainly be observed with regard to immigrant musical and dance performances in the United States. Immigrant dancers and musicians are influenced by their daily life in the United States. Hence, in what many immigrants see as a process of preserving some of their home countries' unique art forms in a new land, in their efforts there also occurs a process of cultural invention. At times explicitly, at other times implicitly, and to varying degrees, immigrant performers incorporate into their art forms elements of American culture, ranging from such wide influences as hip hop, rock, and jazz, to name a few.

Cultural organizations enable immigrants to maintain, reinvent, and re-imagine traditions from the sending society. They also help to strengthen the connections with the country of origin and aid in the social construction of immigrant identities. At the same time, however, cultural organizations and their activities emerge in many ways out of the unique situation of living abroad. There are processes of cultural reinvention that occur here.

Traditions, customs, and practices are changed or develop in different ways from an immigrant's country of birth. Immigrants across the United States have been members of cultural associations for at least two centuries. These organizations have been an intrinsic part of the American cultural mosaic. They help immigrants to imagine themselves and transition to live in a new land.

SUPPORT NETWORKS

There are various nonprofit organizations and agencies, often run by immigrants, that pursue a mission to assist various newcomer communities in their daily life. They run self-help programs and aim to provide support on a variety of issues. Many of these organizations provide translation services to help immigrants who know only limited English. They offer language classes to help immigrants improve their English. They aim to create access to education and health services. They tutor children, help parents negotiate problems that their child might have at school, provide health checks, call doctors, or provide suggestions on what health care people can access. A few specialize in providing small business development. Others help with work-related and other economic issues, such as purchasing a home or investing money.

Various organizations also provide social services and advocacy. Again, others lobby for the political rights of immigrants and against political discrimination, or they provide support with immigration-related issues and other legal services. Various support networks provide services in all or several of these areas, or if they cannot provide support they direct newcomers to agencies that can help them with what they need.

Some immigrant support networks run programs to deal with issues of domestic violence and abuse. They can provide safety plans and services to victims, such as connecting people to housing, public benefits, and legal services needed for divorce, a restraining order, child custody, and other issues frequently related to domestic violence. Programs can also provide peer-counseling by immigrant women who are survivors of domestic violence and now counsel women who are undergoing similar abuse.

Some organizations also run HIV and STD prevention programs. Much of their time and resources are spent on health education and teaching others how to prevent sexually transmitted diseases from spreading. They target at-risk populations and collaborate with local community health centers that often provide free and confidential checkups.

This does not mean that sexually transmitted diseases or domestic abuse are necessarily more pressing issues in immigrant communities. Due to cultural differences and values, linguistic challenges, and a variety of other issues, however, the strategies, skills, and solutions to address these problems in newcomer communities can be quite distinct from those that work in mainstream American society. Thus, it makes sense in many instances to have these issues addressed by specific immigrant support networks that are familiar with a particular community and have a specific set of skills, such as knowing the language and being familiar with a group's culture.

Some support networks help newcomers apply for citizenship. Immigrants who have the status of permanent residents, or green card holders as they are still often called, are eligible to apply for citizenship after five years or more of being in this position. A few nonprofit organizations help permanent residents fill out their applications, but they also provide classes that help immigrants get ready for the interview and the citizenship test that is required of them. They thus assist the applicants in the entire process from the application stage to the swearing-in ceremony as a citizen of the United States.

There are also support networks that run youth and after-school programs. They can provide computer classes, tutorials, and opportunities to play and socialize. Often this is done in an effort to keep youth off the streets, especially in tougher communities. Here middle and high school students face particularly unique challenges. Dropout rates within some immigrant communities can be higher, with relatively few students seeking higher education. Thus, such programs aim at helping foreign-born students and the children of immigrants to excel academically.

Dealing with American schools and the process of interacting with school systems are particular challenges for many immigrants. In many cases language issues exist. Frequently, foreign-born parents do not speak English and therefore cannot communicate with teachers and school officials. There are also cultural barriers, however, as immigrant parents do not necessarily have the cultural literacy to deal with these issues. Many have little education and experience in dealing with the American educational system. Thus, many are understandably wary to take the initiative to inquire about their children's education.

In addition, some immigrant parents and social workers report that parents can sometimes face discrimination and a lack of support from school districts. Some groups attempt to assist immigrants to overcome these issues by translating for them and by providing them with information about how the educational system works in the United States.

They serve as go-betweens among school districts and immigrant parents. They also try to provide other resources and outreach to help immigrant families and their children to succeed at school, through, for example, after-school programs.

Many groups try to assist parents whose children are displaying behavioral issues at school. These problems can be due to typical teenage behavior or peer pressure, but on occasion they can also be related to gang activity and crime in neighborhoods. Social workers in programs often try to help immigrant students and their parents not only at the schools and in people's homes, but also on the streets.

Other support networks specifically focus their work on refugee populations. Given their distinctive experiences, refugees require unique outreach and support programs. Many of the groups that attempt to assist refugee populations, though certainly not all, are church-supported groups. A growing number of them are also run by or employ former refugees. These individuals are familiar with the unique challenges that the refugee communities face, which often stem from the horrific experiences they underwent in their countries of origin.

Many refugees fled mass violence and war, and some continue to live with the memories, trauma, and the legacies of their earlier experiences. For many it still has a significant impact on their daily lives. In many cases, refugees also come from some of the most impoverished countries in the world—where already poor nations have further suffered from years, and often decades, of war that have ruined local economies and infrastructure. Thus, another challenge for immigrant support networks is to assist refugee populations to adjust to and to ease into their new lives in the United States.

Support networks that assist immigrants in their daily life face many challenges. Available funds are rarely adequate, and competition for available resources is stiff. Often, there is generally more demand for services than these agencies can provide. There are other issues as well. Some immigrants are reluctant to use services because they are afraid, they do not want to bother anyone, or they do not know that such organizations even exist.

EDUCATION

Most immigrants recognize that education can play an important role in their daily life and can potentially provide them with improved future economic and material prospects. Parents recognize it and emphasize this to their children. Education can be one of the factors motivating immigrants to move to the United States. Some even chose the location they move to because they know that in particular communities they have access to good school systems and affordable universities.

A Mexican immigrant child in an early development class. Alison Wright/CORBIS.

Public Schools

There is a growing field of scholarly literature that examines the connections between immigration and education. Schooling certainly provides opportunities and promises to immigrants and their children. Yet, much of the scholarship in this area also examines the many obstacles and challenges that immigrants and their offspring face. As with so many other issues discussed in this book, the subject of education and immigration is tremendously complex and should not be over-generalized.

The education of young immigrants and the children of immigrants is a major issue facing the United States. Today an estimated one in five students is the child of an immigrant. Thus, the future prospects and successes of these students is important not only to the individual, but to the overall well being of American society as well. Many educators and researchers underscore that students of immigrant background need to get special academic support in order to assure their academic success, since they often face unique challenges in terms of language and also in terms of their families' different cultural values and understandings.

The academic performance of students who are immigrants or the children of immigrants mirrors that of the general public, ranging from high academic achievers to those who perform poorly. Many of the students on the lower end of the academic scale lack the support network they need to help them to improve their academic performance. These students often live in rough neighborhoods, where crime and poverty compound the cultural difficulties immigrant students already face.

The challenges that immigrant students face often go beyond academics. Some feel great pressure to assimilate into the larger mainstream American culture at school. Naturally, some resist such efforts, and others find themselves in significant identity struggles as the student tries to figure out to which world he or she belongs. Stigmatization and stereotyping is also an issue. Some students come from less privileged backgrounds and face social disparagement in school. In many instances, it is hard for those students to move beyond the preconceived notions and stereotypes held by some in the mainstream.

Such attitudes often impede the positive performance of pupils in the educational process, which in turn shrinks their possibilities for economic and social advancement. In addition, voices in the media along with those of some teachers, peers, and school administrators, help to reinforce the students' negative perception of their place within the academic environment. They may hear, for example, disparaging remarks about immigrant parents not being involved in their children's life at school. Such comments often do not take into consideration that many of these parents have to work two or three jobs, and that oftentimes they also are not comfortable speaking English, in addition to facing several other cultural barriers. Hence, many feel uncomfortable interacting with teachers and school officials.

There also seems to be a gender gap that exists among immigrant students in terms of education. On average, girls and young women are outperforming boys and young men. This is a similar social phenomenon as in mainstream American society. In immigrant communities this development can also be influenced by differences in cultural realities, such as different attitudes about masculinity that exist in some sending societies and that are also embraced by some immigrant children.

Family background frequently plays an important role in a student's academic performance. Generally the children of well-educated parents tend to perform better academically than the ones from poorer families. This, of course does not mean that immigrant students from less affluent backgrounds have no chance to do well academically. It does mean, however, that they have to overcome more challenges in their daily life to do so. Parental involvement with education can be a deciding factor. Furthermore, in the case of first-generation young immigrants, the quality of the educational system of their sending society can also play a role in the academic performance of a student.

While many immigrants and their children have a strong desire to learn English, issues related to language remain a powerful stumbling block in the area of education. There is a low tolerance for bilingualism in the American educational system, and there is concern among some immigrants about their children losing the language of their sending society. Furthermore, the second generation of immigrants for whom English is a second language and whose parents do not have the English skills to support their children's academic efforts can face significant challenges. This can manifest itself in the lack of students' participation in class discussion and especially in their writing. Some experts warn that a failure to address the issues that immigrant students face could create a permanent underclass among those who are being left behind.[23]

Many school administrators, school officials, educators, policymakers, and social workers are aware of the challenges that immigrant students face. They attempt to address these issues through a variety of programs, networks, and initiatives. One school official, who is herself an immigrant, explains:

I think we are doing a lot more to learn about the cultures that are in front of us in the classroom. And I think we are trying to be more sensitive to the needs of our diverse students. Teachers are taking courses and are participating in trainings in order to improve their instructional strategies and to improve their understanding of the students' backgrounds.[24]

School districts, non-governmental organizations, and social agencies try to create systems that assist schools in trying to improve student retention and performance. They make use of translators, social workers, and advocates to obtain these goals by attempting to bring students, teachers, school administrators, and parents together to work toward the goal of improving the public education system for immigrants. Still, it is important to underscore that multicultural diversity and the capability to reach all students effectively are likely to remain challenges for the U.S. educational system for years to come.

Home-Schooling

Home-schooling is an educational alternative that is embraced by some immigrants. In March 2008, for example, the *New York Times* reported on this issue with regard to the Muslim community in Lodi, California. Lodi is a predominantly agricultural settlement 70 miles east of San Francisco. The newspaper writes that about "40 percent of the Pakistani and other Southeast Asian girls of high school age who are enrolled in the district are home-schooled, though broader statistics on the number of Muslim children being home-schooled, and how well they do academically, are elusive."

An English adult learner class consisting of elderly Latino and Russian immigrants. AP Photo/Mike Derer.

Like many American Christians in mainstream society who decide to home-school their children (an estimated 1 million to 2 million), some immigrants of Muslim faith feel that sending their children to schools will have a negative impact on their development. They fear that public education might expose their children to social ills such as drugs, alcohol, violent crime, as well as premarital sex and indecent relationships. A statement made by one Muslim mother who home-schools her children in San Jose, California underscores these views. "Little girls are walking around dressing like hoochies, cursing and swearing and showing disrespect toward their elders. In Islam we believe in respect and dignity and honor."

While in some instances the girls are being kept out of school and are being home-schooled so that they are able to help with chores around the house, efforts to use home-schooling as a means to socially isolate girls in Muslim communities are not generally the norm, but the exception. The Muslim immigrant community in Lodi is quite conservative in its views. "Some 80 percent of the city's 2,500 Muslims," writes the *New York Times*, "are Pakistani, and many are interrelated villagers who try to recreate the conservative social atmosphere back home. A decade ago many girls were simply shipped back to their villages once they reached adolescence."

There are numerous other reasons why some immigrants decide to home-school their offspring. In fact, many dislike the labels that are often imposed on families who decide to home-school their children, including charges that they are "weird," "antisocial," or "religious extremists." Instead, many who pursue this route have concerns about the performance and the mission of public—and also at times private—schools. Others do not have the resources to provide their children with a private education, but believe that they can provide a better education at home than schools provide.

Many people who pursue home-schooling are frustrated with the low test scores produced by the public schools in the communities where they live. Some others believe that by home-schooling their children they can better preserve their home countries' culture and protect their children from what they perceive as some of the negative influences of mainstream culture. There is also often a concern about discrimination. Some immigrant children who are now being home-schooled have been referred to by ethnic slurs and, as a result, have been pulled out of school by their parents. Muslim students in particular can be targeted in public schools and ridiculed for their beliefs and are occasionally called terrorists.

As in mainstream America, the issue of home-schooling is contentious among immigrants. Many fear that home-schooling could unnecessarily isolate their children. They feel that their children should be integrated into the system. Being a student in the public school, they believe, will better prepare and help their children adapt to life in the United States. Facing discrimination in public school, they argue, better prepares their children to deal with the system, and in some cases teaches them a lesson on how to fight for their rights.[25]

STRESS, MENTAL HEALTH ISSUES, AND CULTURE SHOCK

The experience of migration, or prior experiences in their sending societies, can saddle immigrants with stress, mental health issues, as well as culture shock. All these can have an impact on the daily life of at least some immigrants. Refugees from war zones and genocides especially can suffer from posttraumatic stress disorder, which can manifest itself in recurring flashbacks or nightmares of their harrowing experiences as well as in general symptoms of depression.

Non-refugee immigrant populations can be susceptible to stress and mental health issues as well. For example, researchers have found that migrant workers in the agricultural sector have a much higher risk of suffering from depression compared to the general population. Thus, socioeconomic alongside cultural circumstances do have a significant impact on the mental health picture of immigrants.

Immigrants can also be susceptible to "culture shock." Arriving in a new place and adapting to a new culture, norms, and behaviors is not easy. The difficulties of adjusting to life in the United States can manifest themselves in various forms, such as depression. These emotional responses become ways for immigrants to deal with different stages of homesickness, with their unfamiliarity with certain aspects of American culture and life or dealing with their dislikes about how certain things are done in the United States. For the vast majority of immigrants, however, culture shock is a temporary phenomenon, and they adjust to their new surrounding over time.[26]

CRIME

There is a common perception among some mainstream Americans that immigrants are disproportionately involved in crime, and it is a view frequently presented in some media outlets. Much of this presentation has to do with stereotypes, misperceptions, and the politicization of immigration, an issue that is discussed in detail in later chapters. In fact, this has happened throughout American history. In the mid-nineteenth century such allegations were often directed against Irish immigrants, and later in the nineteenth century similar accusations were leveled against Italians.

The "myth" that immigrants disproportionately commit crimes "is not supported by empirical data." In fact, even though the number of foreign-born residents in the United States—both legal and illegal—has dramatically increased since the 1990s, property crime and violent crime have declined significantly. Foreign-born men between the ages of 18 to 39 are five times less likely to be incarcerated than American-born members of this age group.[27]

Furthermore, immigrants are at least as likely to be on the receiving end of crime as they are the perpetrators of it. They can fall victim to violent crime, property crime, and, as discussed in Chapter 5, sometimes even hate crimes. Crime disproportionately occurs in low-income areas, where many of the poorer immigrants live.

FASHION AND DRESS

Reflecting the way that many people around the world dress, immigrants who live in the United States often wear Western-style clothing. Thus, most clothe not very differently from mainstream Americans. Sometimes, however, various types of "traditional" clothing can be worn by immigrants during religious ceremonies, holidays, and family festivities like weddings, but also, in some instances, in their day-to-day life.

The diversity of dress among immigrants often depends on which area of the globe the newcomers arrive from. Some immigrants from Africa, for example, wear clothing items alternatively know as the Dashiki, Boubou, or Agbada. They are worn among people from western Africa and throughout the Sahel Zone. The Dashiki is a very long shirt, often

Various traditional clothing worn by immigrants. Jon Feingersh/Blend Images/
CORBIS.

very nicely ornamented, that reaches down to the calves and is worn over
long pants of the same color. Often it is put on in combination with a hat
or cap. West-African men may also wear a shirt, tailored in various styles
and made of elaborately embroidered or nicely printed linen or cotton.

Some African women wear caftans made of beautiful fabrics often coordinated with a complementary cap or head covering. African women on
occasion wear long dresses or skirts and shirts made out of traditional
African print fabrics, which are often combined with a matching hat or
covering of the same fabric. The long and wavy Bogolan, or mud shirt,
that covers most of the body is an informal version of the West-African
Dashiki. It is not only popular with African immigrant men, but they are
also worn by women.

There is tremendous diversity among Asian immigrants' clothing.
On certain occasions and depending on their sending society, they can
wear "traditional" dresses, robes, kimonos, shirts, suits, saris, and traditional kurta pajamas. Many immigrants of Muslim background, on special occasions such as holidays or festivals, and in some instance in their
day-to-day life, wear a garment called the jellabiya. They are worn by
men and women alike and are cut similarly to the West African Dashiki
discussed above. The jellabiya can be made from simple, inexpensive
materials to nicely embroidered, ornamented, and expensive fabrics.

In addition, some Muslim women choose to cover their heads in their
daily life using a scarf or a wrap. Some also wear a cloth or jacket called

the *jilaabah* that covers their entire body. This way of dressing, along with the head covering, is seen as a sign of modesty by many Muslims.

The wearing of "traditional" clothing and what makes "traditional" dress changes over time and has place-specific meanings. What people in mainstream American society call a "traditional" outfit is often part of the daily life of some people in non-Western societies. Furthermore, the way that some people in the United States believe people dress in certain sending societies is actually based on stereotypes. The idea of "traditional" clothing is thus contested. A third-generation Polish immigrant describes an experience that underscores this issue. Volunteering during a cultural festival, she describes the following encounter with a first-generation immigrant:

We were selling our Polish food. Two of us were in native Polish costume. One of the more recent immigrants went by and waved. Our feeling, to our amusement, was that she would feel uncomfortable in the costume, and that it would represent something that was just so in the past.[28]

Styles and fashion change over time. What "traditional" clothing meant for one generation means a historic period costume that no one would wear for a more recent immigrant.

FOOD

Just like earlier arrivals throughout American history, immigrants who have come in the last few decades are bringing with them their diets, food items, and cooking styles. Food, in the most basic human terms, provides nourishment, sustenance, and enables survival. As mentioned earlier, newcomers can use food as expressions and tools of preserving their ethnicity and identity. Furthermore, adapting to American food can also become a sign of becoming part of U.S. society. Hence, food plays a central role in the daily life of immigrants.

Due to the wide variety of ethnic restaurants that exist, most Americans believe that they have an understanding of immigrant foods. They feel that they are familiar with Mexican diets, such as enchiladas, tostadas, or tacos, or that they know Chinese cuisine because they have eaten at Mexican or Chinese restaurants. These understandings, however, often over generalize the regional complexity and diversity that exists in the diets of such large countries as China or Mexico. Furthermore, American "ethnic" restaurants often cater to American expectations and tastes— thereby changing or Americanizing the food they serve.

The way immigrants eat is more diverse and complex. The dishes that are served in the United States often have been modified because cooks need to use locally obtainable ingredients and cooking methods and cater to changing tastes as well as outside influences that are being picked up while living in a new environment and which are now incorporated into new dishes. For example, immigrant parents often change their cooking styles to accommodate their offspring's tastes. The younger generation experiences new flavors during school lunches or when they visit American-born friends. They are also influenced by advertising, and thus tend to develop different tastes than those of their parents. Oftentimes, too, the decision to change diet can be due to economics. Mainstream American food items are often cheaper and more widely available in stores, and therefore they become more widely used by immigrants as well.

As discussed in Chapter 2, there are entire ethnic stores as well as aisles in mainstream supermarkets that cater to the dietary needs and interests of immigrant populations. The large presence of immigrants in the United States has led to the opening of a wide variety of ethnic restaurants from all regions of the world. Thus, there are not only changes in consumption occurring among immigrants; in turn, mainstream American society is being transformed by the presence of newcomers.[29]

MUSIC

Immigrants have also brought and continue to bring their music. Music can provide a vital link to the sending society. It can help immigrants in their efforts to maintain and reinvent their ethnic identity. At the same time, the music of immigrants also changes and is transformed as the newcomers are influenced by American elements through their life in the United States. Furthermore, globalization and the vast impact of Western popular culture since the 1960s has also influenced the musical styles of many non-Western societies around the world. In turn, rhythms and musical elements used by immigrants also influence American composers and songwriters.

Immigrants perform all genres and types of music. Some play the more traditional "ethnic" or "folk music" of their sending societies. Often these performers attempt to preserve these musical styles because they see them as a vital part of their culture, often with roots dating back to ancient times. The music played by other immigrants is influenced by and ranges from rock to pop to rap music, genres that have a global appeal, and which have been influenced by the music styles originally introduced to the Americas by slaves from West Africa.

Non-American music forms, in some instances introduced by newcomers, have also left their mark on the United States. Reggae, for example, has been an influential style. Hip hop, influenced by reggae and mixed with a fast spoken-sung dialogue, might arguably be even more prominent and is claimed to be the creation of the Jamaican immigrant DJ Cool Herc. Various music and dance styles from Latin America, such as salsa, conga, rumba, and mambo, have also had an influence that reaches beyond the Latino community. Moreover, artists like Gloria Estefan and Ricky Martin have gained mass-market appeal by fusing Latino music styles with pop music elements.[30]

NOTES

1. Diana Eck, "Religion," in *The New Americans: A Guide to Immigration Since 1965*, ed. Mary Waters and Reed Ueda (Cambridge, MA: Harvard University Press, 2007), 214–227.

2. Eck, 215.

3. Peter Occhiogrosso, *The Joy of Sects: A Spirited Guide to the World's Religious Traditions* (New York: Doubleday, 1994), 74.

4. Eck, 215–217.

5. Eck, 215–217.

6. Eck, 217, 219.

7. Jeffrey Gerson, "The Battle for Control of the Trairatanaram Cambodian Temple," in *Southeast Asian Refugees and Immigrants in the Mill City: Changing Families, Communities, Institutions—Thirty Years Afterward*, ed. Tuyet-Lan Pho, Jeffrey Gerson, and Sylvia Cowan (Lebanon, NH: University of New England Press, 2007), 153–172.

8. Bryan Tran interviewed by Christoph Strobel, Craig Thomas, and Yingchan Zhang, May 8, 2008, Ethnographic Study of Lowell, MA.

9. Bryan Tran interviewed by Christoph Strobel, Craig Thomas, and Yingchan Zhang, May 8, 2008, Ethnographic Study of Lowell, MA.

10. Phala Chea interviewed by Christoph Strobel, January 15, 2008, Ethnographic Study of Lowell, MA.

11. Olivia Cadaval, *Creating a Latino Identity in the Nation's Capital: The Latino Festival* (New York: Garland Publishing, 1998), XIV–XV.

12. Cadaval, Chapters 4 and 5.

13. Cadaval, 157.

14. See http://www.lowellwaterfestival.org/ (accessed February 19, 2009).

15. My interpretation here benefited from Cadaval, 5, 13.

16. See Madhulika Khandelwal, *Becoming American, Being Indian: An Immigrant Community in New York City* (Ithaca, NY: Cornell University Press, 2002), 160.

17. Khandelwal, 161.

18. The Association of Indians in America, http://www.aiausa.org (accessed August 11, 2008).

19. Khandelwal, 168–169.

20. Khandelwal, 172–173.

21. Khandelwal, 172–174.

22. Khandelwal, 163–164.

23. Marcelo Suarez-Orozco, Carola Suarez-Orozco, and Irina Todorava, *Learning in a New Land: Immigrant Students in American Society* (Cambridge, MA: Belknap Press, 2008).

24. Phala Chea interviewed by Christoph Strobel, January 15, 2008, Ethnographic Study of Lowell, MA.

25. Neil MacFarquhar, "Resolute or Fearful, Many Muslims Turn to Home Schooling," *New York Times*, March 26, 2008.

26. Alejandro Portes and Ruben Rumbaut, *Immigrant America; A Portrait*, Third Edition (Berkeley, CA: University of California Press, 2006), 178–188.

27. See Edward Sifuentes, "Immigrants Do Not Commit Most Crimes," *The North County Times*, February 26, 2007. http://www.nctimes.com/articles/2007/02/27/news/top_stories/1_02_512_26_07.txt (accessed April 1, 2009).

28. Pauline Golec interviewed by Christoph Strobel, Craig Thomas, and Yingchan Zhang, April 16, 2008, Ethnographic Study of Lowell, MA.

29. James Loucky, "Food," in *Immigration in America Today: An Encyclopedia*, ed. James Loucky, Jeanne Armstrong, and Larry J. Estrada (Westport, CT: Greenwood Press, 2006), 122–125.

30. Bertil van Boer, "Music," in *Immigration in America Today*, 240–244.

5

FACING STEREOTYPES, DISCRIMINATION, AND TENSIONS

Stereotypes, discrimination, and tensions are part of the experience of many immigrants who are sometimes targeted for being "different" by people in mainstream society. Anti-immigrant sentiment can be observed in stereotypical portrayals, which sometimes become apparent in popular opinions, attitudes, and in a range of media outlets. It can also be witnessed in the various forms of discrimination endured by many newcomers to this country. These social phenomena, at least in part, shape the quality of life of immigrants and the views of mainstream American society. They have an effect on whether newcomers feel welcome and on how they adjust to life in the United States.

It is often said that the United States is a nation built by immigrants. Mainstream American society acknowledges the importance that immigration has played in the nation's past. At the same time, the United States still has its fair share of advocates of nativism who dislike immigrants and immigration. Nativists tend to believe that foreign languages, cultures, and customs have a harmful influence on the nation. They want to preserve "America for Americans" and advocate a reduction in immigration.

These are people who often acknowledge their family's immigrant roots but argue that immigration in the past played a constructive role. Their family members came to the United States "legally," learned English, and helped build the country. However, they see the more recent wave of immigration in a very different light. They argue that today's immigrants come from different, non-European cultures and have a destructive impact on the fabric of American society.

Many mainstream Americans disagree with this assessment. In fact, the experiences that immigrants are undergoing today, while in some ways different, are in many ways similar to the experiences of immigrants in the past. Then, as now, immigrants are trying to make it in America. As in the past, immigrants struggle with English as a foreign language and often live in poor, crowded housing. Some seek to assimilate, while others are more interested in earning money and returning to their country of origin. Still others try to maintain as much of their home culture as they can as they begin a new life in the United States.

Like their predecessors of the nineteenth and the early twentieth century, immigrants of the twenty-first century face discrimination. Furthermore, today, as in the past, many immigrants are hardworking and motivated to improve their family's situation. Of course, this description does not fit all recent immigrants, just as it did not fit everyone in the past. The story is more complicated and nuanced. As we have seen, there exists a tremendous diversity among immigrants—not only in terms of race, ethnicity, but also in terms of class, level of education, and social achievement.

ANTI-IMMIGRANT SENTIMENT

The debate about immigration in the United States has been a long-lasting one. The national historical dialogue over the "benefits" or "evils" of immigration, and what to do with what some have called the "threatening waves of foreign migrants," is as old as the country's history. For newcomers to the United States, however, anti-immigrant sentiment often went beyond mere discussions and debates. Throughout the nineteenth and early twentieth century immigrants faced discrimination and tensions. There existed job discrimination, political disenfranchisement, cultural repression, and violent attacks on immigrants and their institutions.

If historically Americans were concerned about the arrival of Europeans, immigrants from the non-Western world, such as China and Japan, faced even harsher discrimination, hostility, and exclusion. Despite their relatively small numbers they faced severe racism. Much of white American society perceived these two groups of immigrants as a threat. Historically, Asian immigration was often referred to as the "yellow peril." In the second half of the nineteenth century there were widely reported beatings, lynching, and killings of Asian Americans.

The level of discrimination and racism facing these groups can be seen in the passage of the Chinese Exclusion Act in 1882, which introduced legislation that, among other things, made it harder for Chinese to come to the United States. Other examples of anti-immigrant sentiment were the internment of approximately 100,000 Japanese Americans during World War II and the passage of the Immigration Act of 1924, which especially limited immigration from countries in the non-Western world.

With the rise of the foreign-born population in the United States in the last few decades, anti-immigrant sentiment among some people has been fueled once again. These attitudes are reflected in a growing literature that advocates for tougher border controls to undermine migration—illegal as well as legal in many cases. Many proponents of this view see immigration as threat to the American way of life—economically, politically, and culturally. Conservative radio talk show hosts, letters to the editors, editorials in newspapers, and various Internet resources reflect this view as well.

Fearing an "Alien Invasion"

Anti-immigration advocates decry any positive impact that immigration might have on the United States. They argue that immigrants take American jobs and negatively influence wages by depressing them downward. A significant share of this sentiment is directed against irregular immigrants. An estimated 11 million to 13 million immigrants without legal papers are believed to live in the United States today. These numbers are of concern to many mainstream Americans who fear that they might lose their jobs because their employees might hire an immigrant who will do the same job for less pay.

There are also concerns that illegal immigrants bring crime to communities, and more recently some anti-immigration ideologues have tried to link immigration to terrorism. Immigrants are also being blamed for threatening America's English-speaking identity, for wasting American tax money on welfare, and for changing the face of America in ways that some critics dislike.[1] The accuracy of many of these claims is widely contested.

Many nativist pundits are especially concerned about the volume of Mexican and Latino immigrants coming to the United States. They argue that irregular immigrants have much higher crime rates—an issue, as discussed in Chapter 4, of significant debate. They also question the allegiance of "millions" of Mexican immigrants who "still retain their loyalty to Mexico and have no desire to learn our language or become part of our family, and many have become militantly ethnocentric."[2]

"We are literally being invaded," writes one commentator, "and our government isn't doing anything about it." The editorial continues:

Thousand of illegals cross our borders each and every day, bringing with them crime, disease and terrorists, and in most cases we have to accommodate their needs; their language, their culture, medical needs, education (bilingual education), illegal driver's licenses ... [which] cause needless deaths on American highways. Worse is that their agenda calls for Mexican immigrants to maintain their own language and culture and their loyalty to Mexico. Why? Because Mexico believes our Southwest— California, Arizona, New Mexico, Texas, Colorado and Nevada—rightfully belongs to them. They plan to occupy these states and make them carbon copies of Mexico. Politically corrupt, teeming with drug runners, [and] poverty.[3]

Such extreme and xenophobic statements do occur frequently, even in mainstream media outlets. They underscore the fact that a considerable number of people in the United States see immigration as a political, economic, and cultural threat to the nation.

As noted in the above quote, bilingual education and English language acquisition causes tension. Scholars of international migration often point out that the United States is less tolerant than other countries of linguistic diversity, and that there is a push for English-only education, for which there is strong support in mainstream America. Immigrants, and especially their children who are educated in public schools in the United States, are pushed to acquire English. Often this comes at a price. Many of the full English immersion programs fail to teach immigrant children English language fluency effectively.

To make matters worse, sometimes immigrant children also lose much of their native language while undergoing English-only language programs. This, ironically, happens at a time when many affluent and upper-class Americans push their children to learn a foreign language because they see potential future gains for their offspring in obtaining such skills.[4]

Anti-immigrant sentiment in the United States can be particularly pronounced when it comes to "bilingual education" and "English-only" programs. A tasteless column, written in what is supposed to be "immigrant English," provides a glimpse at these sentiments: "Sum immigrant groupz think lernin Inglish iz two nationaliztic or patriotik. They wood rather sea kidz bluff there weigh thru skool. A lutt did. Cuz the skoolz let them." The columnist complained that, no "one wantz to lern the langage. No one wantz to make kidz or adultz lern it eyether."

The particularly aggressive tone of the column underscores the strong feelings that some people in the American mainstream have toward foreign language speakers and how to teach those who are different and come from different linguistic backgrounds. According to the writer of this column, there is one solution: English only. He writes, "Why don't they stik two the basiks likte I lernt, frum good teechers who nu Inglish?"[5] The challenges of having to learn, and what it means to live in a new language, as well as the potential benefits that American society gains from having citizens and residents with different language skills, is often lost in this one-sided discussion.

Facing Discrimination and Stereotypes

The attacks on immigrants and expressions of anti-immigrant sentiment in some of the media have real-life implications. Stereotypes and anti-immigrant sentiments expressed in newspapers, on radio talk shows, on Web sites, or on television are reflected in the views of many people in mainstream American society. Some occasionally make open comments about immigrants in public, which can have strong racist connotations.

When people are confronted about utilizing such terms, some claim to not understand the hurtfulness or the meaning of the words they just used. Others justify their remarks by saying: "I am not a racist, but . . . " This implies that it is the presence of immigrants that pushes them to use such harsh words, indicating that the fault is not with that person's racial or ethnic sentiments or hatred, but rather that it is immigrants that should be blamed, and that the offender has legitimate reasons to be angry.

The reasons and roots of anti-immigrant sentiments in mainstream American society are complicated. As mentioned, they go far back in American history. Furthermore, the dislike of immigrants is not a phenomenon that is unique to the United States. In fact, it exists in many societies around the world where significant immigrant populations live.

There are a variety of reasons why some Americans hold such views. It is important to point out, though, that the explanations below are in no way an attempt to justify discrimination against immigrants. Nonetheless, it is important to have a basic understanding of the forces that shape anti-immigrant feeling. It certainly is the case that some people simply dislike change or anything alien and therefore despise the presence of immigrants. For many others, however, the story is more complex. Anti-immigrant sentiment is in many instances spurred by fear.

Many Americans feel that immigrants threaten their position in society. They are afraid that immigrants could take their job or that immigrants are the reason why their salaries are low. Also recall another frequent claim about newcomers: that they are to blame for Americans losing welfare benefits or having to pay more taxes because immigrants supposedly take advantage of or abuse social services. The changing face of neighborhoods and society in general is a further complaint by some mainstream Americans. They feel uncomfortable with their new neighbors, the new businesses, and the new places of worship that are emerging in their places of residence. They feel intimidated by people who often have a different color of skin, speak an unfamiliar language, wear "exotic" clothing, and eat different foods. Thus, immigrants frequently become the scapegoats of people's fears and insecurities. In many instances, the fear manifests itself in openly expressed anti-immigrant sentiment, discrimination, and, as discussed later in this chapter, violence and hate crimes.

Discrimination is often experienced at work. Many immigrants feel that their linguistic ability can be an impediment for job advancement, and they understand that a language barrier can hold them back. At the same time, they feel that employers can hold the fact that they speak with an accent against them. An articulate and well-educated Latino woman who came to the United States in her late teens relates that she was overlooked for a job once for which she had the right qualification and training. The woman who was hired for the job was a native-born American who had little experience and only limited knowledge of Spanish, even though this was a prerequisite for the position.[6]

Some immigrants also wonder if the fact that they are foreign born and speak with accents can impede their chances of receiving a job promotion or a salary increase. Discrimination in the form of taunts can also come from coworkers. Foreign-born colleagues are sometimes accused of "talking funny," And coworkers can also make disparaging remarks about an immigrant's country of origin. Many such comments are intended as a little joke or jab, but they often have a hurtful impact.

Housing discrimination is another issue that immigrants can experience. Due to their accents, some report that they get turned down by certain landlords on the phone before they even get to see an apartment. On other occasions they maintain that landlords do not bother to call them back, even though they left a phone number and times that they can be reached. Ethnic and racial profiling can also happen after immigrants visit an apartment due to the color of their skin or their foreign background. Some landlords are evasive when confronted with such issues. Others claim that a place has already been rented to another person, even though the same property is advertised for rent in the following weeks.

Racial and ethnic profiling as well as stereotypes can occur and pose problems in other parts of the daily life of immigrants or those who are perceived to be newcomers. One interviewee relates two examples of how federal authorities in the upper-scale neighborhood where he lived targeted Mexican Americans, believing that they might be undocumented workers laboring for local families. "I know Chicano doctors who were working in their yards. INS officers came up to them and asked" for their papers. In another incident, he relates, "a doctor's wife was walking to the store. She was stopped by INS agents who asked if she was maid for one of the local doctors."[7]

There are also reports that immigrants or those who are perceived to be newcomers have a harder time getting adequate services or that they face discriminatory practices when they deal with banks or insurance companies, for example. Furthermore, foreign-born citizens have reported that they have been turned away at voting booths or that they had to produce proof of citizenship, evidence that white, American-born voters did not need to provide.

Immigrants can also become the victims of targeted vandalism against their property. One West-African immigrant tells about how his family's property was being repeatedly targeted due to the color of his skin and his immigrant background. The perpetrators threw eggs against his house, left racially charged graffiti, and broke into his family's car several times. Eventually the perpetrators stole the automobile and burned it. This situation made the interviewee feel increasingly insecure in the neighborhood where he, his wife, and children owned a house, and had lived for several years. Police finally became involved when the car was stolen and burned. It took this gentleman and his family a long time to gain back trust in their surroundings, as it was never clear who had committed these vicious acts.[8]

At times discrimination against immigrants can be connected to current events. An Armenian-American woman who came to the United States as a young girl in the 1960s, and frequently is mistaken for being Hispanic or Muslim, explains how during the Iranian hostage crisis, when 53 Americans were taken captive for 444 days in the United States embassy in Tehran, she was on several occasions confronted with screams of "Muslim go home" when she was walking down the streets. At a time when calls to "nuke Iran" frequently heated up nationalist emotions, a severe anti-Muslim sentiment existed among at least some Americans.[9]

Acts of discrimination and racial and ethnic slurs can happen anywhere. It is virtually impossible for immigrants to protect themselves against such insults and attacks. Getting picked on for having darker skin, for having an accent, for wearing different clothing, for speaking a different language, or being called an "illegal" can occur at work, at school, or while walking down the streets.

Discrimination is part of the daily life of many of immigrants. Still, it is important to highlight that many newcomers go to pains to point out that despite unfortunate encounters with anti-immigrant sentiment, they largely have positive encounters with American mainstream society. They generally like their places of residence and are fond of many of their neighbors and coworkers. They try to live fulfilling lives in the United States and work to realize their family's and their own dreams and aspirations.

Moreover, not all immigrants experience discrimination. Some actually point out that the situation in their sending societies was far worse than in the United States. One newcomer from West Africa explains how:

Back in my country I [experienced discrimination]. . . . Here never! But in the Ivory Coast two times. . . . In most African countries there are different ethnic groups. The ethnic group in power controls everything. Those not in power are controlled and are told what to do, and you can't get anything that they don't want you to get. That is the reason why I didn't hesitate to leave the country.[10]

Thus, experiences with discrimination are complex and diverse.

Hate Crimes

Every year, various media outlets across America report hate crimes that target immigrants. These acts and incidents are motivated and fueled by the hatred and fear that some individuals have toward newcomers and the perceived and real change they bring to American society. The perpetrators often feel that violence will somehow change the situation, might scare the newcomers, and might lead them to leave the community.

Reported hate crimes can include the destruction of private property, graffiti with discriminatory messages, defacing of immigrant businesses, verbal and physical assaults, as well as racially or ethnically motivated killings. In Newmarket, New Hampshire in 2002, for example, a member of the Lao community died after one of his white neighbors from his apartment complex assaulted him. The white neighbor had been angry and intoxicated and apparently assaulted the Laotian man because he had allegedly lost a relative during the Vietnam War. He told the police that "what's going on is that those Asians killed Americans and you won't do anything about it so I will. . . . Call it payback."

While a crime of this nature is despicable under any circumstance, the sad irony in this case was that the older Laotian man had fought alongside the Americans during the Southeast Asian wars, when he served in the Laotian army. According to his grandson, he fled Laos after U.S. forces withdrew from Vietnam and when a Communist regime took power in Laos in the late 1970s. He was then granted political asylum in the United States.[11]

The Minuteman and Anti-Immigrant Activism

In the last few years, spurred by fears that the United States is flooded by illegal immigrants, there have been several organizations created that claim they are working toward the goal of stemming the tide of immigration. Some of these groups maintain that they are working through political lobbying, activism, and demonstrations to secure the nation's border. The Minuteman Project, founded by James Gilchrist of Aliso Viejo, California, and the Minutemen Civil Defense Corps, led by Chris Simcox, are the two most notorious groups that have emerged.

Minuteman members lobby politicians to be hard on undocumented immigrants and argue for increased border security and the construction of a border fence. Both groups also actively patrol the borders of the United States. Because of their confrontational activism, especially their guarding of the Mexican-American frontier, several observers have referred to the Minuteman members, and groups that operate in a similar mold, as vigilantes who are taking the law into their own hands.

POST-SEPTEMBER 11 AMERICA

The terrorist attacks of September 11, 2001, had a significant impact on the United States. The events on that day have caused many Americans to reexamine their place in the world, to think about their personal relationship to their country, and to think more about issues of national security. The assault had an impact on many of the country's newcomers as well. Like many Americans in mainstream society, immigrants have also come to reexamine their relationship to the United States. In addition,

Minuteman Project Volunteers observing the U.S.-Mexican border. Fred Greaves/Reuters/CORBIS.

the terrorist attacks have in some cases led to an anti-foreign backlash that targeted specific populations and turned them into scapegoats.

Immigrants and September 11

Since September 11, daily life in many ways has become more challenging for immigrants, especially when dealing with federal authorities. Many observe that it is harder for their foreign relatives to obtain visas to visit them in the United States. The processing of paperwork has significantly slowed down as applicants are more thoroughly vetted. These developments are largely due to heightened security concerns in the United States, but they also reflect the more general concerns among some policymakers about the growing wave of immigrants to the United States. There are concerns that some family members could come to the United States on a tourist visa, and that then they might not return to their home countries and stay behind as illegal immigrants.

Immigrants comment on the extra security checks that they have to go through when they travel by airplane or when they enter government buildings. They have also noticed that there are now stricter controls at the border when they try to enter the country after traveling abroad. Many acknowledge the need for heightened security and welcome it. Some, however, wonder if they are profiled due to their foreign background and are thus more thoroughly checked than their mainstream American counterparts.

Numerous immigrants feel that the events of September 11 connected them more closely to the United States; they believe that it was their home country that was attacked. Thus, terrorist violence not only led many mainstream Americans to rally around the flag in an outpouring of patriotism, but it had the same impact on many immigrants.

Reflective of this view, a Vietnamese American explains that September 11 had a big impact on him. He argued that he was patriotic and appreciative of the United States before the terror attacks, since the country had taken him in as a refugee after he fled Vietnam, but he has become even more grateful now. Since September 11, he has been particularly conscious to buy only American-made cars, and he tries to make an effort to buy as many American-made products as he can. He stated that it was important to keep America's economy strong and the nation powerful, and that he is now making an even more concerted effort to stay more involved and to give back to the country that has given him so much.[12]

September 11, the Muslim American Community, and Other Scapegoats of Hate Crimes

Muslims or people who in the mind of some Americans "look like" Muslims have in particular faced discrimination and tensions. They have been especially targeted in the aftermath of September 11 and have sometimes been turned into scapegoats of misplaced aggression and anger.[13]

Muslim immigrants in the United States have in many ways fared better than those in Europe. Muslim populations there are often of lower or working-class background and frequently live in impoverished parts of cities and towns. They often face open discrimination and are marginalized in society. In the last several decades, violent assaults against Muslim immigrants have occurred widely throughout Europe.

A popular scholar of religion writes that American Muslims, unlike many of their contemporaries in Europe, in general "feel that they are in the United States by choice. They want to become Americans, and in the land of the melting pot integration is more of a possibility than in Europe."[14] Still, it is easy to oversimplify the situation and conditions of immigrants of Muslim faith in the United States. Their situation is not without problems, challenges, and discrimination.

Many Muslim immigrants in the United States are well educated and are of middle-class background. They work as engineers, doctors, and academics. The class diversity among Muslims in the United States is more complex, however, as there are also immigrants from the Islamic world who lead a working-class existence. Thus, while there are many well-educated and well-to-do Muslims in America, there are others who struggle financially.

The situation of Muslim immigrants in the United States changed dramatically on September 11, 2001. On that day 19 hijackers captured four passenger airplanes. They flew two of them into the World Trade Center in New York City, another one into the Pentagon in Washington, D.C., and the fourth crashed into a field in Pennsylvania. The coordinated suicide attacks on September 11 left more than 3,000 people dead. The terrorists who hijacked the planes were affiliated with Osama Bin Laden's Al Qaeda terror network—a radical Sunni Muslim terrorist group that had attacked a variety of Western targets around the world since the 1990s.

While the vast majority of Muslims in the United States and around the world condemned the acts of terrorism committed against the United States, racist and anti-Muslim sentiment erupted after September 11 among at least some Americans. Muslims faced violence and discrimination after the attacks and were too often painted with one brush. As fear and anger dominated popular opinion, at least for some, being a Muslim became synonymous with being a terrorist.

Furthermore, the September 11 attacks became the reason to call for stricter immigration policies. "[T]he United States must get more serious about flushing out and handling these terrorists as well as moving to keep them out of the country," wrote one columnist. "The pressure has to stay on, the investigations have to intensify and we need to seriously consider a moratorium on Muslim immigrants."[15] A similar hostile tone was also taken by several elected federal and state officials, as well as by some evangelical religious leaders like Billy Graham and Pat Robertson.

Media around the country reported various attacks on Muslims, their places of worship, as well as on Arabs and Arab Americans of Christian background, and on other minorities, especially on immigrants from India. Muslims and people who "looked like Muslims" were attacked in the streets, were called names, had their property violated and damaged, and were on several occasions not allowed to board planes. Muslim women were reluctant to wear their traditional dress for fear of retaliatory attacks, being insulted, or being discriminated against. Fears about Islam were spurred by the ignorance by many in mainstream society about the religion, and by the fact that some Americans connected the religion to violence and aggression.

Muslims also experienced discrimination at work, and hundreds of unfair terminations of jobs were reported in the aftermath of September 11. The Council on American-Islamic Relations reported 1,717 incidents that targeted Muslims, and which occurred between the terror attacks through February 2002. This number did not include violence against other groups such as Arabs with Christian backgrounds or people from India, groups that had also been frequently targeted after September 11. Anti-immigrant violence took various forms ranging from vandalism, to assault, to murder.[16]

The private property and businesses of some immigrants did become the target of vigilante attacks. One restaurant owner of Middle Eastern descent described an attack on his café:

Four came smashing in the coffee shop.... They bring a lot of anger with them, throwing with their hand and feet all the tables and chairs bent over to the floor. They break a lot of things. Break the windows, break the mirror and all the glasses. ... There's broken glass all over. Table everywhere. I'm thinking now we are between the two sides. I'm afraid from the terrorists number one, and now I'm afraid from the American too.[17]

Such incidents of vandalism and violent attacks were not uncommon experiences for a good number of immigrants in post-September 11 America.

Several incidents of ethno-violence occurred against Muslims, and some of these hate crimes culminated in murder. Three killings of Muslims occurred in September 2001. The first victim, Waquar Hassan, an immigrant from Pakistan and father of four children, was killed in his grocery store in Dallas. A few days later, Ali Almansoop, an immigrant from Yemen, was murdered in his home in Lincoln Park, Michigan. The third victim, also an immigrant from Yemen and father of eight children, was executed late in September while working in his convenience store in Reedley, California.[18]

After the September 11 attacks, some people who appeared to look Middle Eastern to some bigoted people, but who were not Muslims, also fell victim to acts of racial discrimination and violence. The Sikhs who originate from India were one group that especially felt the wrath of vigilantes. Male Sikhs wear turbans to cover their hair—a religious requirement—which leads some to confuse them with Muslims out of ignorance. Following the assaults on the Trade Towers and the Pentagon, many Sikh Americans and immigrants feared for their safety and worried that mainstream Americans would question their patriotism. Like Muslim Americans, they had to face verbal insults, uncomfortable stares, and physical assaults. Tragically, a Sikh gas station attendant, Balbir Singh Sodhi, was shot on September 15 while at work in Mesa, Arizona, the weekend after the terrorist attacks. Adel Karas, a Coptic Christian of Arab descent, was assassinated in San Gabriel, California while working in his store on the same day. Vasudev Patel, an immigrant from India, was another victim. He was shot dead working in his convenience store in Mesquite, Texas, on October 4, 2001. These hate crimes spurred by misplaced aggression and ignorance left a harrowing legacy for the surviving family members.[19]

Many American citizens, religious leaders, officials, and politicians deplored the assaults that occurred after September 11. Regular citizens held vigils around mosques to protect the buildings. Religious leaders spoke out against violence and pleaded for cooler heads to prevail. Many police superintendents announced that they would persecute any hate crimes based on race or religion. Furthermore, sensing the danger and the damage that anti-Muslim sentiment might cause in the country, President George W. Bush appealed to Americans quickly after September 11, arguing that Islam was "peaceful" and that the hijackers were not representative of the religion. Still, for many immigrants of Asian and Arab background the situation remains tense and concerns and fears over further discrimination and persecution continues.

At times, due to their religious belief, Muslim immigrant and Muslim-American students are called "terrorists" by their classmates in school. While this has been a discouraging and difficult experience for many, some Muslim students have been inspired to learn more about civil rights and careers in law. Others have been moved to actively attempt to educate their classmates about Islam and to provide their peers with a better understanding about their faith.[20]

In one of his routines, the Arab-American comedian Ahmed Ahmed pokes fun at the increased security checks and the ethnic profiling of Muslims in the United States—an all-too-common experience for many in their daily life:

My name really is Ahmed Ahmed, and I can't fly anywhere.... All you white people have it easy. You guys get to the airport an hour, two hours before your flight. It takes me a month and a half. Security has got so bad that I arrive at the airport in a g-string.[21]

This shows that humor becomes a means of resistance against and a means of dealing with discrimination. It becomes a strategy to poke fun at unfair treatment while it humanizes Arab Americans at the same time.

INTER-ETHNIC TENSIONS AND VIOLENCE

Anti-immigrant sentiments are not the only reason why inter-ethnic tension and violence can occur. It would be too simplistic to put immigrants only on the receiving end or as the victims of discrimination and violence. Sometimes immigrants can also discriminate and violently lash out against others. The diverse multicultural makeup of the American mosaic can sometimes lead to ethnically or racially charged situations.

The observations and experiences of a Brazilian man, who is married to a Portuguese-American woman, provide a glimpse of the issue of inter-ethnic tensions. He observed that while Brazilians and Portuguese share a common language and many cultural attributes, in the community where the couple met there existed some frictions between the two ethnic groups, especially in the 1970s and 1980s. "I always say that although we speak the same language and were colonized by the Portuguese, there is an ocean between us. And that ocean is also present in day-to-day life." Thus the couple faced public disapproval and criticism when they married, tensions that have since subsided. Moreover, the same Brazilian who is an active member in the Latino community observed:

I have seen some tensions among different Hispanic community members because of where they are from . . . it was interesting, I went to a few parties and the Puerto Ricans would be upset because they would play cumbia all night which is Columbian music and not Puerto Rican salsa or merengue. Columbians would be upset the next dance because there was merengue and no cumbia, and they would leave and not go to the next party. I don't think that any of the immigrant groups that come from different regions, for example the Africans, they're not yet a cohesive unit. They come from different parts and if they could just say, "We are Africans and we will squabble among ourselves when we are by ourselves, but to the outside world we are united." Or "We are Hispanics, and to the outside world we're going to be united," it doesn't matter if I come from Santo Domingo or come from Puerto Rico or Columbia. We will squabble among ourselves when we're among our family here. But they have not learned how to do that. Even among the Brazilians there is mistrust. Because Brazil is a vast country and people from the southern part of Brazil may not get along with people from the northern part and there's this regional thing. The Portuguese have two soccer clubs, the blue and red, and they don't seem to be able to coexist in a peaceful and productive manner. I say keep the differences in the soccer field, but they bring it outside. From island to island there is a difference. So if they could just forget those regional things and just think I'm Portuguese, or I'm Brazilian, or African and we should be talking and working together. I think you would see a lot of nice things happening in these ethnic communities as opposed to bickering among themselves which weakens their position and therefore they cannot put on a united front to achieve what they really want.

Ethnic, national, and regional tensions thus can have a significant impact in the daily life of immigrants and impede them to advance their interests.[22]

Schools are places where inter-ethnic tensions and violence can break out, and where they are also more likely to be reported, especially compared to inter-ethnic hostilities that might occur on the streets between groups, gangs, or individuals, and which are more likely to be missed by official observers, authorities, and the media. Lafayette High School in Brooklyn had "a long history of racial tensions, particularly aimed at Chinese and South-Asian immigrant students. New immigrant students, who are perceived as weak and less likely to report crimes, often end up victimized."

For example, in March 2004, one Chinese student was insulted with racial slurs, jumped, kicked, and punched by a mob of African-American students with whom he had been in an argument earlier in the day. This was only one of several incidents at the school. During the same school year, just a few months earlier, on November 21, 2003, a

Chinese student was threatened at knifepoint and mugged on campus. A few days after this incident, another Chinese student was beaten up in a fight in the school cafeteria.[23]

Inter-ethnic fights can also be taken to the streets, playgrounds, and athletic fields. In the summer of 2004, for example, the *Boston Herald* reported "an all-out brawl with baseball bats and knives in South Boston ... which left an Asian teen dead, and was sparked by the use of a racial slur, according to witnesses." Before this incident, there had been tensions for weeks between Asian teens, who lived in the Fields Corner neighborhood in Dorchester, and white kids from Boston's Southie neighborhood. The hostilities had manifested themselves during several small fights between the teens before the conflict escalated into a massive fight with bats and knives.[24]

Inter-ethnic tensions and violence can have a dramatic impact in the daily life of teenagers. They can influence educational success rates and an individual's future. One immigrant tells of his experience in high school. At his institution it was not unusual for students of different ethnic backgrounds to get into fights. African Americans were fighting Hispanics, and the small group of Brazilians to which this student belonged was targeted by both groups. After 10 months he dropped out of school because of the stress as well as the constant need to leave school early and to move around cautiously on campus to dodge attacks.

Such conditions made it virtually impossible to focus on getting an education, and the institution provided little support to students and did not pursue measures to curb the violence. To no surprise, less than a handful of students of a group of 20 to 30 Brazilians actually graduated from that school. In his particular case, there was a happy ending. The interviewee later earned a graduate equivalency degree and went to college. But many others do not have such determination, luck, or the opportunity to finish their education.[25]

NOTES

1. Samuel Huntington, *Who Are We? The Challenges to America's National Identity* (New York: Simon and Schuster, 2004).

2. Patrick Buchanan, "The Balkanization of America: What's My Problem with Mexican Immigration," *Boston Globe*, March 10, 2002.

3. Robert Daigle, "U.S. Is Being Overrun with Illegal Immigrants," *Lowell Sun*, April 17, 2008.

4. Alejandro Portes and Ruben Rumbaut, *Immigrant America: A Portrait*, Third Edition (Berkeley, CA: University of California Press, 2006), Chapter 7.

5. Jim Campanini, "Just Let Kidz Lern Inglish on There Own," *Lowell Sun*, August 15, 2003.

6. Anonymous 5 (Latina) interviewed by Christoph Strobel, April 1, 2008, Ethnographic Study of Lowell, MA.

7. Cesar Caballero, "Chuppies," *The New Americans: An Oral History*, ed. Al Santoli (New York: Viking, 1988), 288.

8. Gordon Halm interviewed by Christoph Strobel, January 16, 2008, Ethnographic Study of Lowell, MA.

9. Muriel Parseghian interviewed by Christoph Strobel, December 7, 2007, Ethnographic Study of Lowell, MA.

10. Emile Tabea interviewed by Christoph Strobel, January 16, 2008, Ethnographic Study of Lowell, MA.

11. "Police Probe Racial Rage in Beating Death," *Lowell Sun*, July 17, 2002.

12. Tony Mai interviewed by Christoph Strobel, April 25, 2008, Ethnographic Study of Lowell, MA.

13. Michael Welch, *Scapegoats of September 11: Hate Crimes and State Crimes in the War on Terror* (New Brunswick, NJ: Rutgers University Press, 2006).

14. For this basic comparison of European and American Muslim immigrants, see Karen Armstrong, *Islam: A Short History*, Revised Edition (New York: Random House Books, 2002), 176–177.

15. Stanley Crouch, "Let's Get Serious on Immigration," *Lowell Sun*, May 6, 2002.

16. Welch, 64–70.

17. Labib Salama and Nasser El Gabry, "Labib's Café," in *Crossing the Boulevard: Strangers, Neighbors, Aliens in a New America*, ed. Warren Lehrer and Judith Sloan (New York: Norton, 2003), 322.

18. Welch, 68–69.

19. Welch, 63, 68–69.

20. Neil MacFarquhar, "Resolute or Fearful, Many Muslims Turn to Home Schooling," *New York Times*, March 26, 2008.

21. Ahmed Ahmed quoted in *Reel Bad Arabs: How Hollywood Vilifies a People*, Jack Shaheen, Media Education Foundation, 2006.

22. Francisco Carvalho interviewed by Christoph Strobel, January 23, 2008, Ethnographic Study of Lowell, MA.

23. "Asian Students Hit in Rash of HS Attacks," *New York Daily News*, March 10, 2004.

24. "Blood Feud: Asians Blame Southie Kids in Fatal Brawl," *Boston Herald*, July 13, 2004.

25. Willian Ferreira Fahlberg interviewed by Christoph Strobel, February 13, 2008, Ethnographic Study of Lowell, MA.

6

POLICY AND POLITICS

Politics and immigration policy shape the daily life of immigrants in considerable ways. Engaging with these issues is of vital importance. Many immigrants, just like numerous mainstream Americans, do not necessarily like to preoccupy themselves with such matters. Yet, regardless of one's level of political participation, policy and politics play a significant role in the lives of immigrants, as it is these policies that shape the options and opportunities open to newcomers in this country.

Immigrants and immigration are significantly impacted by the policies of the U.S. government. The changes that have occurred in this area since the 1960s have spurred the growth of the immigrant population in the United States. As census data suggests, the foreign-born population in the 1980s was 14.1 million people strong. It grew to 19.8 million in 1990 and to 31.1 million by 2000. In the mid-2000s it reached an estimated 37 million.[1]

Thus, as the increasing number of foreign-born people who live in the United States suggests, the relatively more open policy that the federal government has pursued in the last few decades, especially compared to the nation's policy from the 1920s through the mid-1960s, led to a significant demographic shift. If we considered the children of those first-generation immigrants as well, the numbers would be even higher. Immigration policy, often strongly supported and lobbied for by various economic and political interest groups, has spurred dramatically the new wave of immigration in the United States in the last few decades. Rather than providing a complete discussion of U.S. immigration policy, this chapter focuses on several specific pieces of legislation that had an impact on the daily lives of immigrants.

Political strategists and commentators have for some time acknowledged the growing strength and the importance of naturalized immigrant voters. Pundits frequently analyze and comment on the powerful impact that Latino and other immigrant voters will have in the future of American politics, especially as this segment of the population is growing through immigration and naturalization. The second part of this chapter examines the political life of immigrants. It explores the challenges that newcomers face to participate in the political process and the kind of activism they pursue to work toward obtaining their goals.

UNITED STATES IMMIGRATION POLICY FROM 1965 TO SEPTEMBER 11, 2001

The Immigration and Nationality Act of 1965

The Immigration and Nationality Act of 1965 was a significant landmark in the more recent history of immigration policy in the United States. The act led to a significant rise in immigration. It augmented family unification and aided in opening the United States up to more refugees. It also increased visa quotas per country, phased out national origins quotas, and did away with the racial preferences that had existed previously. These developments benefited areas in the non-Western world, especially in Latin America and Asia. The generosity of the act should not be overstated, however. It certainly created boundaries and imposed limits to immigration from the developing world. Furthermore, the Immigration and Nationality Act of 1965 certainly did not keep up with the demand and desires for American visas.

Immigration Laws from the 1970s to 2000

Since the passage of the Immigration and Nationality Act of 1965 policymakers in the United States continued to pursue immigration reform that has had an impact on the daily life of immigrants. The Immigration Reform and Control Act of 1986 (IRCA), for example, tried to devise ways to cut down on irregular migrants by making it illegal for employers to knowingly hire immigrants without papers. The law established financial penalties for employers and required them to complete an Employment Eligibility Verification Form (I-9).

The law also provided a reprieve to some 2.7 million irregular immigrants who had lived in the United States continuously since 1982 by providing them with legal status and the possibility to apply for citizenship in the future. Critics of IRCA have since argued that the immigrants were provided "amnesty" by the legislation. They also maintain that the law had failed to effectively tackle irregular immigration, which has continued, and is believed to have increased, since 1986.

The Immigration Act of 1990 significantly extended the number of people who could immigrate to the United States. It lessened restrictions on the family members of foreign-born Americans and permanent residents to come to the United States, thereby uniting many families. It also provided refugees from war-torn countries provisional protected status. The Immigration Act of 1990 also created H-1B visas, which allowed American businesses to employ highly skilled foreign workers on a temporary basis, thus making it easier for corporations to tap into new sources of labor.

In 1996, Congress passed the Illegal Immigration and Immigrant Responsibility Act. The act "reduced legal immigrants' eligibility for federal benefits such as food stamps and welfare payments, raised the income requirements for sponsors of immigrants, and simplified the process for deporting illegal immigrants and those convicted of committing crimes." It also "placed restrictions on the eligibility of legal immigrants to receive public assistance such as food stamps and Supplemental Security Income, and increased restrictions on public benefits for illegal immigrants."

The welfare cuts hit retired permanent residents especially. In many cases they had lived, worked, and paid taxes in the United States for decades. Thus, many critics of the Illegal Immigration and Immigrant Responsibility Act felt that the reforms unjustly targeted and punished people who had contributed to the system for much of their lives. In part due to pressures and complaints, some—but by no means all—of the benefits taken by the Illegal Immigration and Immigrant Responsibility Act were restored to legal immigrants in the following years, and Congress called its actions "overly harsh."[2]

IMMIGRATION POLICY SINCE SEPTEMBER 11, 2001

The attacks on the United States by terrorists on September 11, 2001, have had a profound impact on the country's immigration policy. They have led to dramatic changes in the structure of the agencies that deal with immigration, have heightened government concerns about security, and have had a significant impact on the daily life of many immigrants.

Homeland Security and the Debate about Immigration Reform since 2001

After September 11, 2001, the federal bureaucracy underwent significant structural changes, and since then there has been a newly invigorated discussion about immigration. Much of the current dispute centers on the familiar economic, political, and cultural issues that have accompanied the debate for decades. Now, however, whether the threat is real or perceived, immigration also has been connected by some policymakers and pundits to the spread of terrorism, and it is seen by some as threatening America's national security.

The months and years after the terrorist attacks on September 11 witnessed a significant restructuring of how the United States administers immigration affairs, which indirectly influenced the daily life of some immigrants. In March 2003, the Immigration and Naturalization Service (INS) was terminated and morphed into three new agencies. The first was the U.S. Citizenship and Immigration Services (USCIS). This agency administered among other things services to people seeking asylum, permanent residence, and naturalization. It was initially referred to as the Bureau of Citizenship and Immigration Services (BCIS).

The second agency that was created is called Immigration and Customs Enforcement (ICE). As discussed later in this chapter, the ICE is in charge of the enforcement of immigration law in the United States. The third agency is the U.S. Customs and Border Protection (CBP). Its responsibilities include border security. While the INS was historically under the jurisdiction of the United States Department of Justice, the three new agencies became part of the newly created Department of Homeland Security.

Throughout the presidency of George W. Bush, immigration policy was a heavily debated issue. President Bush had made immigration reform a key campaign issue during his run for the White House in 2000. When he assumed office in 2001 it became a major policy goal of his administration. In January 2004, Bush proposed:

[A] new temporary worker program to match willing foreign workers with willing U.S. employers when no Americans can be found to fill the jobs. The program would be open to new foreign workers and to the undocumented men and women currently employed in the U.S. This new program would allow workers who currently hold jobs to come out of hiding and participate legally in America's economy while not encouraging further illegal behavior.[3]

Furthermore, in the fall of the same year a bill was introduced to Congress that would permit irregular immigrants living in America to enter a guest worker program. This bill also gave workers the opportunity to apply for permanent residence in the future. In 2005 and 2006, there were several more immigration bills that were introduced to Congress, most of which dealt with different ways of creating a guest worker program for the United States. Some proposals attempted to provide irregular migrants with the ability to gain eventual citizenship after a trial period and after paying a fine provided that they had a clean criminal record, paid their back taxes, and had proficiency in English.

Other plans provided migrant guest workers only temporary access to the United States for a limited number of years, but would require participants in this program to leave after their time was up. The policy discussions reflected the strong disagreement and rift in the debate among politicians and policymakers about immigration issues. They provide a glimpse at the sometimes erratic treatment of foreign-born citizens, legal aliens, and immigrants during this period, which is discussed in more detail below.

The proposed Development Relief and Education for Alien Minors Act (DREAM Act) was part of the effort to reform the immigration system in the first decade of the new millennium. The act attempted to provide high school students or people with a graduate equivalency degree who were undocumented, and who met a set of certain requirements, to be able to attend college or to serve in the armed forces.

The immigrants would have to produce proof that they had lived in the United States since the age of 15 or younger. Initially they would receive temporary permission to stay in the country, and after successfully fulfilling their requirements within a set six-year limitation period they would gain legal permanent resident status. If the immigrant failed to fulfill the set requirements, he would face deportation. The DREAM Act was debated in 2007, but given the anti-immigrant climate in the United States at the time, and due to pressures from conservatives, this legislative piece never passed.

The Border Protection, Antiterrorism, and Illegal Immigration Control Act of 2005 was a plan promoted by conservative members in Congress. Passed on December 16, 2005, the act pushed authorities to crack down on and criminalize irregular immigrants and the businesses that hired them. It also called for the construction of a border fence.

Several of the above-mentioned policy proposals for immigration reform provide hurdles to many immigrants and have an impact on their daily life. The requirements to leave the country for extended periods, for example, are not feasible options for many undocumented immigrants who have strong roots in the United States and would prefer to maintain their illegal status rather than to leave the country. Still, the debate about immigration reform gave many at least some hope that their situation and their status might improve.

A significant number of undocumented migrants dream that they might one day transition out of their undocumented immigrant status. Yet, despite President George W. Bush's ambitious agenda, and Congress's frequent debates in this area, the president's administration and the legislative branch were largely ineffective in bringing about viable reform. The Obama administration, which has been in office since 2009, has so far not been successful on advancing this issue either, despite promises to do so.

Raids and Detention

After September 11, 2001, and especially since immigration became a hot-button issue in the election campaigns of 2004, 2006, and 2008, there has been an increase in immigration raids by authorities in search of undocumented migrants. Once immigrants are arrested they are brought to immigration detention centers, where they are detained and in most cases eventually deported. In such instances, policy has a very direct impact on daily life. Yet, this is not a new development. In the last few decades raids by federal officials have gone through waves. They have ebbed and flowed, often reflecting the political climate on immigration that existed at that time.

Deportations of migrants have occurred widely in post-World War II America. One of the most dramatic episodes occurred in 1954 during the so-called "Operation Wetback." According to immigration officials, hundreds of thousands—and according to some estimates, more than 1 million people—largely of Mexican background, were deported. The majority of deportees were immigrants, but some were also Mexican Americans who were expelled under false premises. The program also cracked down on American employers who hired undocumented immigrants and imposed sanctions against them.

"Operation Wetback" instilled fear in many of the migrants and Mexican Americans who lived in the United States. In fact, the INS claimed that in addition to those who had been arrested and deported, hundreds of thousands of irregular migrants left the country out of fear of being caught by the authorities, but the agency likely overstated these figures for public relations reasons. The mid-1950s was a period of anti-immigrant and xenophobic feelings in the country, and harsh government rhetoric had popular appeal. Even if there were fewer arrests, deportations, and people leaving the country than the government claimed, one should not underestimate the impact that the raids had on the psyche of the immigrant community.[4]

As the debate over immigration heated up again in post-September 11 America, immigration raids have also increased. They especially have been spurred by the Border Protection, Antiterrorism, and Illegal Immigration Control Act of 2005. Since its passage, major immigration raids are frequently reported in the media. Early in March 2008, a widely publicized raid occurred in New Bedford, Massachusetts. Here, 300 federal immigration agents with air support from helicopters raided the premises of a leather manufacturer and arrested around 350 employees. The undocumented workers were principally from Guatemala and El Salvador. According to media reports, the company produced handbags and leather goods and had almost $100 million worth of U.S. military contracts making military backpacks and survival vests. The *Boston Globe* reported that the "indictment accused the company's owner . . . of having knowingly and actively hired illegal immigrants to expand" the work-force from what had been 85 workers in 2003 to about 500 workers at the time of the raid. Authorities also alleged that the owner and "manage-ment staff knowingly" accepted fake documents, and "that they also instructed illegal immigrants on how to obtain fake documents."[5]

In the aftermath of the raid, some members of the public voiced con-cerns about the rapid detention of immigrants in New Bedford and the separation of families that it caused. In many cases the parents who were detained at work were separated from their children at home. Further-more, many of the undocumented immigrants who were arrested on that day were sent to detention centers far away from Massachusetts, making it hard for family members to visit or to reconnect with their loved ones.

Similar raids of equal magnitude have occurred all over the United States. Several ICE raids have targeted the meatpacking industry in the West and Midwest. Raids have also targeted other food manufacturers and restaurants, and thousands of immigrants have been arrested and deported, or face deportation in the future.

The issue of deportation creates significant stress in the daily life of immigrants and their families. The fear of being deported, or of having a loved one sent out of the country, is a constant reality for many illegal ali-ens, who have children, spouses, and relatives who are legal residents or citizens of the United States. It is a traumatic scenario. The sharp increase in arrests and resulting deportations of illegal immigrants since 2005 has augmented the anxieties among undocumented immigrants and their family members. An American citizen who is married to an irregular immigrant from Mexico and who lives in Waukegan, Illinois, a suburb north of Chicago, described her feelings when she talked to the *New York Times*. "It makes me sick to my stomach" with fear, said the woman, every time her husband leaves the house. "I'm like, 'Oh my God, he took too long'.... I'll start calling. I go into panic." In Waukegan, thousands of undocumented migrants and their families have withdrawn from public life. In recent years this has become a national phenomenon. The *New York Times* writes that

[f]rom Illinois to Georgia to Arizona, these families are hiding in plain sight, to avoid being detected by immigration agents.... They do their shopping in towns distant from home, avoid parties, and do not take vacations. They stay away from ethnic stores, forgo doctor's visits and meetings at their children's schools, and postpone girls' normally lavish quinceaneras, or fifteenth birthday parties. They avoid the police, even hesitating to report crimes.

One undocumented Mexican migrant in Waukegan who works in a fac-tory in the area told the newspaper, "When we leave in the morning we know we are going to work.... But we don't know if we'll be coming home."[6]

The raids and deportations of irregular immigrants have not been without critics. Some argue that this is not a feasible strategy or solution to the problem because it does not undermine irregular immigration and comes at too high of a human as well as financial price, both of which far outweigh any benefits. Some commentators argue that this approach panders to political constituencies that want the federal government to get tough on immigration. From the available data it is hard to gage if raids and deportations really curtail irregular immigration, as many migrants still seem to be coming to America despite the crackdown. Once deported, many immigrants head back to the United States in an effort to restart their lives again. Immigration raids can tear families apart, as some relatives have papers and others do not. Thus, the desire to reconnect with their loved ones provides further incentives, alongside economic considerations, for at least some deported migrants to head back north to cross the border as soon as they can.[7]

Furthermore, due to the growing pressure to clamp down on illegal immigration, many legal residents and foreign-born citizens, especially in the Latino community, complain that they are more likely to be targeted in immigrant raids. They are much more likely to be asked to show their papers. Many also believe that discrimination has increased, and they feel that they are being racially or ethnically profiled because white Americans do not have to undergo the same kind of security checks.

A particularly dramatic case of ethnic profiling occurred with Pedro Guzman, a 30-year-old mentally disabled American citizen. He was deported in May 2007, after being arrested on a misdemeanor trespassing charge some time before. On several occasions Guzman tried to return to the United States, but he was repeatedly turned back at the border, while his family tried to find him for almost three months. He was finally found and reunited with his family in August. Guzman's brother Michael told the media: "I will never forget what Peter looked like when he finally returned to the U.S.—exhausted and in terrible shape. . . . Peter's life is forever changed by what his government did to him." Officials with ICE, on the other hand, argue that this was a "one-of-a-kind case." They maintain that the division successfully deported "more than 1 million illegal immigrants" since its creation. Guzman filed a suit against the Department of Homeland security in late February 2008.[8]

There have been other challenges to the immigration raids by ICE. In New Jersey, lawyers based in Newark at the Center for Social Justice at Seton Hall Law School questioned the law enforcement methods used by federal immigration agents in various searches. The lawyers filed a lawsuit on behalf of 10 plaintiffs, two of which were American citizens and the rest legal residents, which accused ICE agents of using "deceit or, in some cases, raw force" to gain "unlawful entry" to people's residences. While immigration officials have the right to question foreigners about their immigration status, they are not allowed to enter a person's home without a tenant's or a homeowner's consent or a warrant. Allegedly, ICE agents either posed as police officers in pursuit of criminals to obtain access, or forced their way in to residences without the necessary papers and then proceeded to detain various individuals.[9]

The conditions in detention centers, which are spread all over the United States, are in many ways comparable to prisons. Illegal immigrants and people waiting for their asylum hearings make up the vast majority of inmates. Detainees are put into small cells and wait for their situations to be resolved.

The substantial increase of the detainee population after September 11 has led to various problems, accompanied by hidden human costs, as federal authorities seemed unprepared to deal with the wave of new arrests caused by the new policies. Conditions are extremely crowded and often unsafe as an ever-growing number of people await their deportation or a hearing with a judge. There are serious staffing shortages at detention centers. The detainees' access to attorneys is also limited. According to the *Washington Post*, only 1 in 10 has a lawyer. The newspaper writes that the "detainees have less access to lawyers than convicted murderers in maximum-security prisons and some have fewer comforts than al-Qaeda terrorism suspects held at Guantanamo Bay, Cuba. But they are not terrorists. Most are working-class men and women or indigent laborers who made mistakes that seem to pose no threat to national security." To make matters worse, detained immigrants can be

A detention center. Jose Cabezas/AFP/Getty Images.

moved from one facility to another without prior knowledge or notification to their family members or their legal council.[10]

There has also been some discussion and criticism about the quality of the medical care provided to detained immigrants. Some critics argue that detained migrants, due to their illegal status, should not be provided with high-quality health care. However, the issues discussed by policymakers seem to be more about setting some adequate mandatory health care standards for detained immigrants. Furthermore, some elected officials argue that deaths at detention centers should be reported to the Justice Department. Congresswomen Zoe Lofgren of California is a main advocate on this issue. "This is about whether the government is conducting itself according to the basic minimum standards of civilization," Lofgren said. The debate has been spurred by a series of articles published in the *New York Times* in May 2008. According to the newspaper, it has obtained a list of 66 named detained dead persons from ICE. Since this story broke, ICE admitted that 71 immigrants died in its custody from January 2004 to early May 2008. A particular tragic incident was that of Boubacar Bah, a Guinean man in his fifties who died while being detained by the authorities. Bah suffered from "a skull fracture and multiple brain hemorrhages," while at a detention center in New Jersey. Apparently Bah was left without any medical care for over 14 hours in an isolated cell. Another case is that of Francisco Castaneda, a detained illegal immigrant from El Salvador. For 11 months he was denied a biopsy while in detention despite doctor's recommendation that he should have one. When he finally received treatment, his cancer had metastasized. He died on February 16, 2008, leaving behind a 14-year-old daughter.[11]

Crime and Deportation

The political debate about immigration also has its impact on the American penal system. Immigrants convicted of crimes make up an estimated 10 percent of the entire prison population. While this figure seems high at first, it is comparatively lower than the number of actual foreign-born people living in the United States, which is estimated at 11 percent to 12 percent. Currently, the yearly figures of immigrant inmates who can be deported, according to United States government officials, range around 300,000. The issue of how to deal with immigrant prisoners has caused some discussion. The *New York Times* writes on this issue:

In the intensely contentious debate over immigration, one point that generally draws broad agreement is that federal authorities should deport illegal immigrant criminals as swiftly as possible. But considerable confusion prevails about how fast that might be. Immigrants convicted of crimes—including illegal immigrants and those who had legal immigration status at the time of the crimes—must serve their sentences before they can be deported. Many immigrant convicts are natural-ized United States citizens who are not subject to deportation.

At a period in American history when there is a noticeable anti-immigrant backlash and a growing sentiment about needing to be tough on crime, there are calls to streamline the process, but also to be strict with immi-grants. Many immigrant rights activists argue that the deportation of legal immigrants is a violation of their human rights. There are reported cases of immigrants agreeing to plead guilty for crimes that they did not com-mit, or to plea bargain for a lesser charge, not realizing, and often without receiving legal counsel, that this decision could lead to their deportation. Furthermore, some of the felonies committed are rather minor—raising some criticism that the crime does not necessarily fit the punishment.[12]

What these numbers, as well as the legal and political arguments, fail to reveal is the tremendous social impact that deportations can have on the daily life of immigrants. It often tears entire families apart. Mothers and fathers have their sons and daughters deported, and children whose father or mother was arrested and convicted lose their parent. If relatives choose to follow a loved one back to the sending society, then deportation can uproot an entire family. The people who face deportation are in many cases from a lower socioeconomic class. Their parents had little under-standing of the American political and legal system, and thus lacked the knowledge, language skills, and often the monetary resources to change their children's legal status. When these children turn 18, they are also often unaware of their situation, or in some cases are apathetic about it, until they are arrested and realize that it is too late. Many immigrants, who may not be de jure, or legally, citizens of the United States, are de facto or culturally American. In those cases, deportation means that they are torn from the county where they lived most of their life, and which they consider their home, only to be sent to a place where they sometimes have never lived, where they do not speak the language well, and where they may experience severe culture shock.

Deportation and the Transnationalization of Gangs

While the phenomenon of the transnational spread of gangs should not be blamed solely on the U.S. immigration policy, the deportation of migrants by authorities has contributed to the growth of gangs around the world. American gangs have especially proliferated in Central America but have also emerged in the last decade or so in parts of South-east Asia, the Azores, and other places. In part, this has to do with the global appeal of American popular culture, which is broadcast around the world in movies and popular music. The images of American gang life and crime, which are celebrated by certain type of media, appeal to certain people around the world. They encourage some to emulate the ways and practices of gangs and apply them to their local circumstances.

The deportation of immigrants from the United States has also had a significant impact on this trend, as it has aided in the export of criminal culture, gangs, and crime. It has, for example, enabled the transnational spread of gangs like Mara Salvatrucha, also known as MS-13. "There was no MS in El Salvador, Nicaragua, and Honduras before the deportation started," explained one of the journalists involved with the documentary film *Explorer: The World's Most Dangerous Gang*. Deported members of the gang usually headed right back to the United States. "But because deportation started to happen on such a widespread scale, these guys started wreaking L.A.-style havoc in their respective countries." Early in 2006, MS-13 subsidiaries were believed to not only exist in 33 states in the United States, but also in six foreign countries. The transnational spread of gangs is believed to have grown since then.[13]

The fact that gangs have been strengthening their position internationally has also helped their stance in the United States, reinforcing the transnational character of their enterprise. Criminal investigators allege that the leaders of gangs like those of MS-13 in El Salvador have strong connections with those in the United States. MS-13 and other gangs impose a rule of terror over the areas that come under their control, whether they are situated in the United States or in Central America. In the United States, gangs like MS-13 are not only active in urban areas as was the case in recent history, but they are also increasingly present in suburbs and even rural areas. "There's evidence that the model of the gang is rape, kill, control," said a U.S. Attorney. "They're really about gaining control over other immigrants from their community, intimidating people and asserting some degree of threat which enables them to control their neighborhoods."[14]

POLITICS

While federal and state policies have influenced and shaped the daily life of many immigrants, politics and political activism provide foreign-born residents with more direct access to the American system, enabling them to directly influence the political process. Still, and for various reasons, there is some reluctance among many newcomers to become politically engaged. For others, however, political participation and activism has become a central part in their daily life.

Political Participation

Like many Americans who were born in the United States, a lot of the foreign-born residents do not care or do not have much time to dedicate to politics. Many lead overscheduled lives. They worry about paying their mortgage or making their rent, they work hard, some are active in their churches or cultural organizations, and they want to spend time with their families and relatives. Such a situation makes it hard for foreign-born citizens and residents to become involved and informed.

Immigrants' view of politics in many ways mirrors that of numerous Americans in mainstream society. Some feel that politics are boring. Others are skeptical about politicians and their ability to bring about change. They feel more often than not that politicians only have their own interests in mind, and care little about the struggles of foreign-born residents. Others feel that they do not have the political literacy to deal with such matters, meaning that they do not know how the system works in the United States. They are unaware of the politicians who are representing them, the candidates who run for office, the political parties that are active in their region, the electoral system, and numerous other topics that they would need to know to be active participants in the process. Again, it is important to reiterate that the newcomers' experience in this regard is not unique, and that many mainstream Americans are similarly uninformed about many of these issues.

Immigrants, however, face a variety of additional trials to their political participation when compared to mainstream Americans. The issues are complex and there are no straightforward answers or models that can be applied. The ethnic, racial, class, and personal backgrounds of immigrants are too diverse to be easily categorized. Furthermore, just because a person acquires his or her citizenship, this does not automatically mean that they will be politically involved. There are various reasons for this. Some newcomers speak only limited English. Many have not gone through the American education system and therefore never learned about the way politics work in the United States. Furthermore, some immigrants and refugees who came from societies that had repressive political regimes may be fearful of becoming too politically engaged due to their previous experiences in their sending societies.

Political participation and citizenship are not only issues of grave concern in the daily lives of immigrants, but they are also of vital importance to American society. In 1950, about 80 percent of foreign-born residents were American citizens. In 2004, however, the number was less than 40 percent. Some speculate that these numbers indicate that this generation of immigrants is less interested in citizenship as well as political participation, and that they are tied less to the United States for various reasons. Some experts, however, argue that it is federal policies that make it harder for immigrants to obtain citizenship and to participate politically, especially when comparing the United States with other societies where there is an official push toward integration of newcomers, such as Canada. There are problems that emerge from low levels of citizenship and political participation. Many newcomers might be left behind by the American system, end up at the bottom of the social ladder, and remain politically, economically, and culturally vulnerable.[15]

There have been some limited efforts to make it easier for foreign-born citizens to be involved in the political process. Some towns, cities, and election districts, for example, provide campaign literature and ballots in foreign languages. While helpful to some larger immigrant communities, these attempts cannot help all, especially given the wealth of languages that are spoken by immigrants in the United States. Thus, many naturalized Americans and experts feel that more resources need to be dedicated and provided to make the political process more accessible. A good number of foreign-born citizens believe that some politicians do not necessarily bother to, or could do more to, reach out to them as voters. Despite an expressed willingness, many immigrants simply do not know how to learn more about the political system and where they would need to go to access that kind of information. Others simply do not care to achieve political literacy.

On the other hand, there are many immigrants who overcome the challenges to be politically engaged. Some believe it is imperative to be politically active and to have their voices heard. They are critical of immigrants who stay out of politics, and hope that, in the future, others will be more engaged in local, state, and national politics. It is, however, harder for foreign-born citizens to get elected to higher office, as they often do not have the financial resources to stage a successful campaign.

Furthermore, in some instances mainstream Americans and even immigrant voters of a different community can be reluctant to vote for a

A person signs in before attending a community neighborhood meeting in Wichita, Kansas. AP Photo/Larry W. Smith.

candidate that might be typecast as an immigrant candidate due to their racial or ethnic background. In addition, in the last two decades there have been frequent allegations of voter discrimination that target foreign-born voters. Communities, towns, and cities throughout the United States have been accused of drawing districts or wards in ways that discriminate against ethnic and minority voters. Critics argue that these actions have led to the de facto disenfranchisement of many foreign-born voters.

Transnational Politics

Foreign-born residents are not only involved in the politics of the United States, but at times they can also participate in what some scholars call "homeland politics" or "transnational politics." This social phenomenon means that foreign-born residents can, for example, donate money to political parties and candidates of their liking in their sending societies. Furthermore, they can also try to influence the situation abroad by involving themselves in, or by lobbying the United States government on behalf of, their countries of origins.

On occasion, expatriates can also hold demonstrations in America, protesting, for instance, a sitting government or certain human rights abuses in their countries of origin. In the Cambodian community in the United States, for example, some people support political parties in their sending society such as the Cambodian People's Party (CPP), the Royal Party, or the Sam Rainsy Party. While it is a minority among Cambodian Americans who participate in such transnational politics, in the city of Lowell, Massachusetts, for example, squabbles between party activists have on some occasions prevented collaboration on initiatives that might have benefited the immigrant community there.

However, this phenomenon is increasingly generational, as one Cambodian American man explains, especially as immigrant communities become established in the United States. "The elderly, the older population, the males, they are thinking of homeland politics. The younger generation, my generation, tends to think more of the politics here." However, the interviewee also points to the challenging road ahead that many, especially the economically disadvantaged groups, face in the United States. "There's really a long way to go.... The way to see it is that Cambodian Americans still have a very low social and economic status. Therefore they are unable to put into, or adapt to, or use the existing infrastructures, the political structure in the United States for the benefit of the community."[16]

Political Activism

Political activism among immigrants has played a central role in American history in the nineteenth and early twentieth century. It has continued to do so in the post-World War II period. In the 1940s, 1950s,

1960s, and 1970s as part of the greater civil rights movement, Americans of Hispanic and Asian descent, alongside African Americans and Native Americans, struggled for full citizenship rights and against racial discrimination. These struggles have inspired many immigrants in their political activism to push toward greater equality.

In the 1960s and 1970s, the efforts of Cesar Chavez and the National Farm Workers Association, later renamed United Farm Workers, are often cited as playing a pivotal role in the Mexican-American civil rights struggle. Chavez was an American of Mexican descent, a farm worker, and a labor organizer who helped to register Mexican Americans in California to vote and to fight for their civil rights. The movement inspired other Hispanics in the Southwest to become active in the struggle. Underscoring the complexities in ethnic relations, however, the Mexican-American struggle in the Southwest and California also revealed economic and ethnic tensions. During the strikes, Chavez and the United Farm Workers protested that growers used irregular immigrants as strikebreakers and revealed their identities to the authorities. The union often saw irregular migrants as a potential threat to its efforts in organizing workers and to the economic well-being of its members.

In their political activism, immigrants have protested federal and state policies. For example, Proposition 187, which was passed in California in 1994 and which attempted to reduce illegal immigration by denying irregular immigrants public services, was opposed by many newcomers. As the media widely reported at the time, tens of thousands of immigrants in California protested prior to this measure. Some pundits at the time argued that the demonstrations, which were accompanied by the display of Mexican flags, led to increasing anti-immigrant sentiments in California and aided in the passage of the statewide initiative.

Nevertheless, in the long run Proposition 187 hurt its political advocates. Its successful passage angered many foreign-born voters, who in the following election decided to vote against those politicians who had proposed and supported the initiative. It was a strong display of the potential power that immigrant voters can have at the ballot box when they feel their position is threatened.

Manifestations of immigrant political engagement and activism have been demonstrated by the "A Day Without an Immigrant" marches that took place for the first time on May 1, 2006. Hundreds of thousands, maybe as many as 1 million, immigrants went to the streets in American cities all over the country. March organizers maintained that protesters came out in as many as 70 metropolises. Cities like Chicago, Los Angeles, Miami, Las Vegas, Phoenix, Denver, Washington, D.C., Milwaukee, Atlanta, San Francisco, and New Orleans were sites of especially sizeable demonstrations. The largest protests occurred in the Los Angeles and Chicago metropolitan areas, where according to some estimates as many as 200,000 to 400,000 people took to the streets.

"A Day Without an Immigrant" protest march in Los Angeles, May 1, 2006. Lucy Nicholson/Reuters/CORBIS.

Despite these sizeable numbers, the protests were well organized and peaceful. *CNN.com* described the scenes in many American cities on that day. "Kids skipped school. Men and women walked off their jobs. Others didn't bother going to work. Businesses shut down for lack of patrons or employees." According to the *New York Times*, the roots of the boycott grew from an idea hatched by a small band of grassroots advocates in Los Angeles who were inspired by the farm worker movement of the 1960s led by Cesar Chavez and Bert Corona. Through the Internet and mass media catering to immigrants, they developed and tapped a network of union organizers, immigrant rights groups, and others to spread the word and plan events tied to the boycott, which were timed to coincide with International Workers Day.

"A Day Without an Immigrant" marches have been held since 2006 on every May 1. While the numbers of protesters in these later events were still impressive, attendance has been smaller. Fear of persecution and arrest is a major reason why the number of protesters has steadily declined.[17]

The economic effect of the "A Day Without an Immigrant" marches is hard to gage. The protests, most economists believe, did not have a long-term or harmful impact on the American economy. It is clear, however, that many businesses lost revenue on the days when the boycotts occurred. Many immigrant rights activists argued that these losses underscored the crucial contribution that immigrant laborers and consumers play in the United States.

In 2006, because they feared financial losses, several employers threatened their employees that they should show up to work and not to participate in the protests, or they would face repercussions. The effectiveness of these threats is hard to assess, but given the high participation rate in the boycott, it was probably limited. Other companies and managers, however, expressed their support for the marches. They accommodated their employees' wishes and negotiated with them to develop ways they could take time off work to participate in the marches. In some instances, employers even allowed pro-immigration petitions to be passed around in their businesses.

Through the "A Day Without an Immigrant" marches, the demonstrators attempt to influence the political process in a positive way. Organizers of the 2006 boycott hoped that their activism would influence the debate about immigration and would push Congress to pass favorable legislation for immigrants. The main goal was to achieve immigration reform. During the marches, demonstrators usually held American flags and those of other countries and a variety of signs that advocated for immigrant rights.

The placards, which immigrants carried in the various protests from 2006 to 2008, send a clear message. They proclaimed such slogans as "My Dream—the American Dream," "We are America," "We are here to stay," and "We want justice." During the demonstrations on May 1, 2008, there was also a growing number of signs protesting the significant increase in raids and deportations that have accompanied the federal government's crackdown on immigrants in post-September 11 America.

While many immigrant groups supported or were sympathetic toward the goal of the "A Day Without an Immigrant" marches, some groups spoke out against the boycott. In 2006, for example, a coalition of Latino groups held a news conference emphasizing that the protesters did not represent the opinions of all Hispanics. Some critics in various communities argued that the marches were not the right strategy to advocate for immigrant rights, and they feared that the protests might send the wrong signal or might be misinterpreted by people in mainstream American society. Others maintained that pushing Congress toward action on immigration reform might be a more constructive avenue to work toward reform.

Many people in the American mainstream disliked the fact that immigrants demonstrated. They argued that the demonstrations were a display of ingratitude and that undocumented immigrants should not be in the country. They also complained that the immigration reforms demanded by many of the protesters who participated in the "A Day Without an Immigrant" march in 2006 would give undocumented immigrants a chance to obtain legal status and would amount to what anti-immigration reformers call "amnesty."

Some have also alleged that too many demonstrators waved Mexican, El Salvadoran, and the flags of other countries. This has led some critics to question the loyalty of the protesters to the United States. Responding to such criticism, in subsequent "A Day Without Immigrant" marches, demonstrators have made an effort to display more American flags.[18]

NOTES

1. Alejandro Portes and Ruben Rumbaut, *Immigrant America: A Portrait*, Third Edition (Berkeley, CA: University of California Press, 2006), XVI.

2. Rayna Bailey, *Immigration and Migration* (New York: Facts on File, 2008), 55–56.

3. "Fact Sheet: Fair and Secure Immigration Reform," January 7, 2004, http://www.whitehouse.gov/news/releases/2004/01/20040107-1.html (accessed April 14, 2008).

4. David Reimers, *Still the Golden Door: The Third World Comes to America*, Second Edition (New York: Columbia University Press, 1992), 59.

5. Yvonne Abraham, "Up to 350 in custody after New Bedford immigration raid," *Boston Globe*, March 6, 2008.

6. Julia Preston, "Facing Deportation but Clinging in U.S.," *New York Times*, January 18, 2008.

7. "Immigration: Not Very nICE," *The Economist*, April 26, 2008, 46, 48.

8. Greg Risling, "Southern Californian Sues Over Wrongful Deportation," February 27, 2008, *Journalgazette.net*. http://www.journalgazette.net/apps/pbcs.dll/article?AID=/2008-227/APA/80227099&template=apart (accessed April 30, 2008).

9. Julia Preston, "Lawsuit Challenges Immigration Raids in New Jersey," *New York Times*, April 4, 2008.

10. Dana Priest and Amy Goldstein, "System of Neglect: As Tighter Immigration Policies Strain Federal Agencies, The Detainees in Their Care Often Pay a Heavy Cost," *Washington Post*, May 11, 2008.

11. Nina Bernstein and Julia Preston, "Better Health Care Sought for Detained Immigrants," *New York Times*, May 7, 2008.

12. Julia Preston, "304,000 Inmates Eligible for Deportation, Official Says," *New York Times*, March 28, 2008; Priest and Goldstein, "System of Neglect," *Washington Post*.

13. Gloria Goodale, "L.A.'s Latest Export: Gangs," February 10, 2006, csmonitor.com. http://www.csmonitor.com/2006/0210/p15s01-altv.html (accessed April 4, 2008).

14. Piers Scholfield, "The World's Most Dangerous Gang," April 3, 2008, *BBC News*. http://news.bbc.co.uk/go/pr/fr/-2/hi/americas/7328967.stm (accessed April 4, 2008).

15. Irene Bloemraad, *Becoming a Citizen: Incorporating Immigrants and Refugees in the United States and Canada* (Berkeley, CA: University of California Press, 2006).

16. Samkhan Khoeun interviewed by Susan Thomson and Christoph Strobel, January 8, 2008, Ethnographic Study of Lowell, MA.

17. Ines Ferre et al., "Thousands March for Immigrant Rights," May 1, 2006, *CNN.com*. http://www.cnn.com/2006/US/05/01/immigrant.day/index.html (accessed May 30, 2008); Randal Archibold, "Immigrants Take to U.S. Streets in Show of Strength," *New York Times*, May 2, 2006.

18. Ferre et al., "Thousand March for Immigrant Rights"; Archibold, "Immigrants Take to U.S. Streets in Show of Strength."

EPILOGUE: A GLIMPSE
AT THE FUTURE

Politicians, media pundits, and public commentators for some time now have
debated whether immigrants are undergoing a process of "integration"
into American society. Some argue that immigrants are assimilating into
mainstream society and that the United States is benefiting from the wave of
newcomers. Others, however, are critical of the impact of global migration on
the United States. They maintain that the new arrivals are causing an
economic drain on the country and are not becoming "Americanized" at all,
or at least not quickly enough. Such observers tend to see the long-term presence of immigrants in America as harmful and threatening.

Researchers and writers with a scholarly interest in immigration argue
about the issue of integration as well, though the debate is generally less
politically loaded. Some academics embrace an intellectual framework
that is called "assimilation theory." They define "assimilation as the
decline of an ethnic distinction and its corollary cultural and social differences." They argue that like previous generations of immigrants from
Europe, the newer generations of immigrants from Latin America, Asia,
and Africa are becoming part of and are indeed "remaking the American
mainstream."[1]

Other scholars of recent immigration to the United States argue that the
experiences of immigrants are too varied to generalize them into this one
theoretical model. They point out that in an "increasingly heterogeneous
American society" there are "multiple alternative options for immigrants
and their offspring." They maintain that while many immigrants "strive to
learn English and incorporate themselves into their new environment . . .

the forms in which they do are so diverse as to render any notion of a uniform assimilation process untenable."[2]

Academic concepts like assimilation, integration, or adaptation try to encapsulate complex and diverse economic, social, cultural, and political processes. How and to what degree do newcomers become part of mainstream society? What are their connections to their country of birth, and how does this relationship in turn define their attitude to their country of residence? How does a person self-identify? How do group dynamics and ethnic communities shape these processes? What role does the reception and perception of immigrants in mainstream society play? These are just a few compelling questions that need answering in order to understand such academic organizing principles.

Trends and processes related to the daily life of immigrants in the United States will need to be observed for some time to get clearer answers to these questions. Some proponents of assimilation theory are certainly right to remind us that it took earlier immigrants decades to blend into American society. Although historic comparisons can provide valuable insights into certain trends and tendencies, history does not necessarily repeat itself. The situation today could be quite different from the developments that have occurred in the past.

As we have seen, communication technology and travel make it easier for many immigrants to stay connected with their home countries. How the processes of what we today describe as "globalization" and "transnationalism" will impact immigrants is hard to gauge at this point. An introductory examination of the daily life and the experiences of immigrants, such as this book provides, simply cannot adequately tackle such questions and theories. It provides, however, a preliminary glimpse of the tremendous complexity and diversity in the lives and communities of immigrants in the United States.

Immigrant identities and national loyalties are extremely fluid and complex. Frequently individuals and groups disagree on or interpret such issues quite differently, which complicates the meaning of such concepts. Undergoing certain processes or doing specific things might be seen by one person as "integrating" into American society, but not so by another. Furthermore, a person could provide answers that to them would mean that they have become part of the mainstream, but which would not be seen in that way by another person.

Newcomers often provide what some would describe as "contradictory" answers to questions of identity and belonging. It is important to remember, however, that many of us have not only national, but also regional, local, religious, family, and many other identities. For immigrants this becomes even more complex because cultural and social issues are that much more challenging. Different languages, dress, customs, beliefs, as well as more complex and often transnational family relations are only a few major variables that complicate these issues.

Does practicing a certain religion or speaking a different language other than English disqualify you from being an American? Certainly mainstream society defines these parameters of belonging through public attitudes, policy, and law, though these definitions and opinions are diverse, complex, and often contradictory. Furthermore, the notion of who is an American also depends on the personal definition of the immigrant.

A citizenship ceremony. AP Photo/Phelan M. Ebenhack.

Notions of assimilation, adaptation, or integration may or may not have to be reexamined for the latest generation of immigrants that have come to the United States in recent decades and for those who continue to arrive. Their situation, circumstances, needs, and challenges might be different from those of older generations in some ways and might be quite similar in others. The above-mentioned terms may or may not encapsulate the processes of transformation that immigrants are undergoing today. Maybe in the future new academic theories, concepts, and organizing principles will emerge that describe or capture the experience of immigrants.

As we have seen throughout the book, a preliminary survey of daily life in the United States provides some interesting insights into how immigrants are participating in social processes of preservation, but also of reinvention, creation, and recreation of traditions, ways of life, and culture. While immigrants continue some of their established "old ways," they are likewise being altered by living in the United States and being exposed to America's culture, practices, and values. Thus they are undergoing some complex social processes. They often become characterized as "ethnic" Americans who have complex-hyphen-hybrid-group-identities and consist of members of diverse class, cultural, and on occasion racial backgrounds.

It is hard to predict the future dynamics of international migration to the United States and the world. Historians, by nature of their discipline, are particularly reluctant to predict future developments. Still, a book that leads up to the present, and which is in many ways a very "presentist" work, needs to, albeit briefly, contemplate this issue.

There could be a crackdown on immigration in the future. This development could be due to strong anti-immigrant currents in public opinion among some in the United States, sentiments that are accompanied by forceful demands to curtail the flow of newcomers. Such views, especially if they increase in popularity, could lead to efforts by the government to dramatically cut down on the number of immigrants allowed into the nation. It happened in the United States in the first decades of the twentieth century, and similar trends and policy enforcements could materialize again.

Worsening global economic conditions, especially in countries in the Western world, might also curtail immigration from poorer countries in the years to come, as would a greater degree of global equality between the world's richer nations and its poorest. Such developments would take away the economic incentives to migrate for people who live in less affluent countries. At this point, however, our planet's global inequality seems to be increasing rather than decreasing.

As we have seen throughout the book, it is not only immigrants who are changing through their encounter with the United States. Immigration has and will continue to change the face of America in the future.

Projections of the U.S. Census Bureau in 2008 suggest that "minorities" in America might become the "majority" of the population by 2042. Hispanics, African Americans, Asians, and American Indians are forecast to make up 54 percent of the overall populace by 2050. Hispanics and Asians are expected to see especially significant increases. Their population share is predicted to double to 30 percent for Hispanics and to 9 percent for Asians. The acceleration of these demographic developments is estimated to be the result of immigration and higher birth rates. The white non-Hispanic populace is believed to decrease from its current share of 64.7 percent to 46 percent. The estimates also forecast an increase in the number of Americans who are identified as "mixed race."[3]

These projections are of course based on current immigration, birth, and death rates, and as such they have to be considered with some caution. There are a variety of reasons why these demographic developments could not materialize in the way they were forecast. Since the data is based on a prognosis, it cannot account for potential future economic, political, and health factors that might lead to significant alterations. For example, a noticeable decline or a massive increase in immigration could significantly skew these numbers. Equally, a major global pandemic or economic crisis could have a significant altering impact. Nevertheless, the U.S. Census Bureau's 2008 predictions point to important demographic trends. The forecast makes clear that the face of the American mosaic is becoming transformed and that immigration plays a major role as a driving force of these changes.

No matter what future trends will bring, the post-1965 immigration has had and is still having a momentous impact on the United States as immigrants are helping to reshape the country. Without a doubt, immigrants have changed and are changing the United States in significant ways.

NOTES

1. Richard Alba and Victor Nee, *Remaking the American Mainstream: Assimilation and Contemporary Immigration* (Cambridge, MA: Harvard University Press, 2003), 11.

2. Alejandro Portes and Ruben Rumbaut, *Immigrant America: A Portrait*, Third Edition (Berkeley: University of California Press, 2006), 263.

3. "Minorities Set to Be U.S. Majority," August 14, 2008, *bbcnews.com*. http://news.bbc.co.uk/go/pr/fr/-/2/hi/americas/7559996.stm (accessed August 14, 2008).

BIBLIOGRAPHY

MEDIA SOURCES

bbcnews.com
Boston Globe
Boston Herald
cbsnews.com
Christian Science Monitor
Des Moines Register.com
Forbes.com
Journalgazette.net
Lowell Sun
National Public Radio (npr.org)
Nationmedia.com
NEA Higher Education Advocate
New York Daily News
New York Times
Slate.com
South Florida Sun-Sentinel.com
The Economist
Washington Post

OFFICIAL WEB SITES

http://www.whitehouse.gov

DOCUMENTARIES

The Lost Boys of Sudan. Megan Myland and Jon Schenk. Actual Films/Principe
    Production. 2004.
Monkey Dance. Julie Mallozzi. ITVS. 2005.
Reel Bad Arabs: How Hollywood Vilifies a People. Jack Shaheen. Media Education
    Foundation. 2006.

INTERVIEWS

Ethnographic Study of Lowell, MA. Transcripts available at the Center for Lowell
    History in Lowell, Massachusetts.
11/8/2007: Rita Ofori-Frimpong interviewed by Susan Thomson and Christoph
    Strobel.
12/7/2007: Muriel Parseghian interviewed by Christoph Strobel.
12/11/2007: Tooch Van interviewed by Susan Thomson and Christoph Strobel.
12/14/2007: Anonymous 1 (Indian) and Anonymous 2 (Indian) interviewed by
    Christoph Strobel.
1/8/2008: Samkhann Khoeun interviewed by Susan Thomson and Christoph Strobel.
1/10/2008: Bowa Tucker (formerly Anonymous 3) interviewed by Christoph Strobel.
1/15/2008: Phala Chea interviewed by Christoph Strobel.
1/16/2008: Gordon Halm interviewed by Christoph Strobel.
1/16/2008: Emile Tabea interviewed by Christoph Strobel.
1/17/2008: Sidney Liang interviewed by Christoph Strobel.
1/23/2008: Francisco Carvalho interviewed by Christoph Strobel.
2/5/2008: Osvalda Rodrigues interviewed by Christoph Strobel.
2/13/2008: Willian Ferreira Fahlberg interviewed by Christoph Strobel.
2/26/2008: Maristela Tosato interviewed by Christoph Strobel.
2/29/2008: Ana Suarez interviewed by Christoph Strobel, Craig Thomas, and
    Yingchan Zhang.
3/12/2008: Anonymous 4 (Indian) interviewed by Christoph Strobel.
3/14/2008: Halleh Mahini interviewed by Christoph Strobel.
3/15//2008: Blong Xiong interviewed by Christoph Strobel.
3/28/2008: Lisa Dagdigian interviewed by Christoph Strobel.
4/1/2008: Anonymous 5 (Hispanic) interviewed by Christoph Strobel.
4/7/2008: Margarita Turcotte Zapata interviewed by Christoph Strobel.
4/15/2008: Sambath Bo interviewed by Christoph Strobel.
4/24/2008: Ivette Nieves interviewed by Christoph Strobel and Yingchan Zhang.
4/25/2008: Tony Mai interviewed by Christoph Strobel.
4/30/2008: Thong Phamduy interviewed by Christoph Strobel.
5/2/2008: Anonymous 6 (Polish) interviewed by Christoph Strobel and Yingchan
    Zhang.
5/8/2008: Bryan Tran interviewed by Christoph Strobel, Craig Thomas, and
    Yingchan Zhang.

PRINT SOURCES

Abelmann, Nancy, and John Lie. *Blue Dreams: Korean Americans and the Los Angeles
    Riots*. Cambridge, MA: Harvard University Press, 1995.

Abraham, Nabeel, and Andrew Shyrock, ed. *Arab Detroit: From Margin to Mainstream*. Detroit: Wayne State University Press, 2000.

Acosta-Belen, Edna, and Carlos Santiago. *Puerto Ricans in the United States: A Contemporary Portrait*. Boulder, CO: Lynne Rienner Publishing, 2006.

Adams, Leah, and Anna Kirova. *Global Migration and Education: Schools, Children and Family*. Hillsdale, NJ: Lawrence Erlbaum, 2006.

Adler, Rachel. *Yucatecans in Dallas, Texas: Breaching the Border, Bridging the Distance*. Boston: Allyn and Bacon, 2004.

Alba, Richard, and Victor Nee. *Remaking the American Mainstream: Assimilation and Contemporary Immigration*. Cambridge, MA: Harvard University Press, 2003.

Alexander, June Granatir. *Daily Life in Immigrant America, 1870–1920*. Westport, CT: Greenwood Press, 2007.

Alumkal, Anthony. *Asian American Evangelical Churches: Race, Ethnicity, and Assimilation in the Second Generation*. New York: LFB Scholarly Publishing, 2004.

Amaney, Jamal, and Nadine Naber, ed. *Race and Arab Americans Before and After 9/11*. Syracuse, NY: Syracuse University Press, 2007.

Anderson, Wanni, and Robert Lee, ed. *Displacements and Diasporas: Asians in the Americas*. New Brunswick, NJ: Rutgers University Press, 2005.

Annerion, John. *Dead in Their Tracks: Crossing America's Desert Borderlands*. New York: Basic Books, 2003.

Ansari, Maboud. *Iranians in the United States: A Case Study of Dual Marginality*. New York: Associated Faculty Print, 1988.

Appadurai, Arjun. *Modernity at Large: Cultural Dimensions of Globalization*. Minneapolis: University of Minnesota Press, 1996.

Archdeacon, Tomas. *Becoming American: An Ethnic History*. New York: Free Press, 1983.

Armstrong, Karen. *Islam: A Short History*. Revised Edition. New York: Random House Books, 2002.

Arthur, John. *Invisible Sojourners: African Immigrant Diaspora in the United States*. Westport, CT: Praeger, 2000.

Attlee, James. *Isolarion: A Different Oxford Journey*. Chicago: University of Chicago Press, 2007.

Ba-Yunus, Ilyas, and Kassim Kone. *Muslims in the United States*. Westport, CT: Greenwood Press, 2006.

Bailey, Rayna. *Immigration and Migration*. New York: Facts on File, 2008.

Baker, Reginald, and David North. *The 1975 Refugees: Their First Five Years in America*. Washington, DC: New Trans Century Foundation, 1984.

Bales, Kevin. *Disposable People: New Slavery in the Global Economy*. Berkeley: University of California Press, 2004.

Bao, Xiaolan. *Holding Up More than Half the Sky: Chinese Women Garment Workers in New York City, 1948–1992*. Urbana Champaign: University of Illinois Press, 2001.

Baron, Dennis. *The English-Only Question: An Official Language for Americans?* New Haven, CT: Yale University Press, 1990.

Bean, Frank, and Gillian Stevens. *America's Newcomers: Immigrant Incorporation and the Dynamics of Diversity*. New York: Russell Sage Foundation, 2003.

Bean, Frank, and Marta Tienda. *The Hispanic Population of the United States*. New York: Russell Sage Foundation, 1987.

Behdad, Ali. *A Forgetful Nation: On Immigration and Cultural Identity in the United States*. Durham, NC: Duke University Press, 2005.

Bender, Thomas. *Nation Among Nations: America's Place in World History*. New York: Hill & Wang, 2006.

Bergquist, James. *Daily Life in Immigrant America, 1820–1870*. Westport, CT: Greenwood Press, 2007.

Bernal, Martha, and Phylis Martinelli, ed. *Mexican American Identity*. Mountain View, CA: Floricanto Press, 2005.

Beserra, Bernadete. *Brazilian Immigrants in the United States: Cultural Imperialism and Social Class*. New York: LFB Scholarly Publishing, 2003.

Bloemraad, Irene. *Becoming a Citizen: Incorporating Immigrants and Refugees in the United States and Canada*. Berkeley, CA: University of California Press, 2006.

Bodnar, John. *The Transplanted: A History of Immigrants in Urban American*. Bloomington, IN: Indiana University Press, 1985.

Bonacich, Edna, and Richard Appelbaum. *Behind the Label: Inequality in the Los Angeles Apparel Industry*. Berkeley, CA: University of California Press, 2000.

Borjas, George. "Economic Theory and International Migration." *International Migration Review* 23 (1989): 457–485.

———. *Friends or Strangers: The Impact of Immigrants on the U.S. Economy*. New York: Basic Books, 1990.

———. *Heaven's Door: Immigration Policy and the American Economy*. Princeton, NJ: Princeton University Press, 2001.

Bowe, John. *Nobodies: Modern American Slave Labor and the Dark Side of the New Global Economy*. New York: Random House, 2007.

Brimelow, Peter. *Alien Nation: Common Sense about America's Immigration Disaster*. New York: Random House, 1995.

Buchanan, Patrick. *Death of the West: How Dying Populations and Immigrant Invasions Imperil Our Country and Civilization*. New York: St. Martins Griffin, 2002.

Burns, Roger. *Cesar Chavez: A Biography*. Westport, CT: Greenwood Press, 2005.

Cadaval, Olivia. *Creating a Latino Identity in the Nation's Capital: The Latino Festival*. New York: Garland Publishing, 1998.

Canniff, Julie. *Cambodian Refugees' Pathways to Success: Developing a Bi-Cultural Identity*. New York: LFB Scholarly Publishing, 2001.

Caplan, Nathan, Marcella Choy, and John Whitmore. *Children of the Boat People: A Study of Educational Success*. Ann Arbor, MI: University of Michigan Press, 1991.

Castles, Stephen, and Mark Miller. *The Age of Migration: International Population Movements in the Modern World*. Third Edition. New York: The Guilford Press, 2003.

Chan, Sucheng, ed. *Hmong Means Free: Life in Laos and America*. Philadelphia: Temple University Press, 1994.

———. *Not Just Victims: Conversations with Cambodian Community Leaders in the United States*. Urbana-Champaign, IL: University of Illinois Press, 2003.

———. *Survivors: Cambodian Refugees in the United States*. Urbana-Champaign, IL: University of Illinois Press, 2004.

———. *The Vietnamese American 1.5 Generation: Stories of War, Revolution Flights and New Beginnings*. Philadelphia: Temple University Press, 2006.

Chavez, Leo. *Shadowed Lives: Undocumented Immigrants in American Society.* San Diego: Harcourt Brace Jovanovich, 1992.

Chin, Ko-Lin. *Smuggled Chinese: Clandestine Immigration to the United States.* Philadelphia: Temple University Press, 2000.

Chiswick, Barry. *The Economics of Immigration.* Northampton, MA: Edward Elgar, 2005.

Cieslik, Thomas, David Felsen, and Akis Kalitzidis. *Immigration: A Documentary and Reference Guide.* Westport, CT: Greenwood Press, 2008.

Cohen, Robin. *Global Diasporas: An Introduction.* Seattle: University of Washington Press, 1997.

———. *Migration and Its Enemies: Global Capital, Migrant Labor, and the Nation State.* Aldershot, VT: Ashgate Publishing, 2006.

Conover, Ted. *Coyotes: A Journey Through the Secret World of American's Illegal Aliens.* New York: Vintage, 1987.

Copeland-Cortes, Jacqueline. *Creating Africa in America: Translocal Identity in an Emerging World City.* Philadelphia: University of Pennsylvania Press, 2004.

Cortes, Carlos, ed. *Cuban Exiles in the United States.* New York: Arno Press, 1980.

Crane, Ken. *Latino Churches: Faith, Family, and Ethnicity in the Second Generation.* New York: LFB Scholarly Publishing, 2004.

Cross, Malcolm, and Robert Moore. *Globalization and the New City: Migrants, Minorities and Urban Transformations in Comparative Perspective.* Houndmills, England: Palgrave, 2002.

Daniels, Roger. *Asian America: Chinese and Japanese in the United States Since 1850.* Seattle: University of Washington Press, 1989.

———. *Coming to America: A History of Immigration and Ethnicity in American Life,* Second Edition. New York: Harper Collins, 2002.

———. *Guarding the Golden Door: American Immigration Policy and Immigrants Since 1882.* New York: Hill and Wang, 2004.

Das, Mitra. *Between Two Cultures: The Case of Cambodian Women in America.* New York: Peter Lang, 2007.

Deaux, Kay. *To Be An Immigrant.* New York: Russell Sage Foundation, 2006.

Diner, Hasia. *The Jews of the United States, 1654–2000.* Berkeley: University of California Press, 2006.

Dufois, Stephane. *Diasporas.* Translated by William Rodarmor. Berkeley, CA: University of California Press, 2008.

Durand, Jorge, and Douglas Massey, ed. *Crossing the Border: Research from the Mexican Migration Project.* New York: Russell Sage Foundation, 2006.

Ebaugh, Helen Rose, and Janet Saltzman Chafetz, ed. *Religion and the New Immigrants: Continuities and Adaptations in Immigrant Congregations.* Walnut Creek, CA: Alta Mira Press, 2000.

Ehrenreich, Barbara, and Arlie Russell Hochschild. *Global Women: Nannies, Maids, and Sex Workers in the New Economy.* New York: Holt, 2004.

Espinosa, Gaston, Virgillio Elizonodo, and Jesse Miranda, ed. *Latino Religions and Civic Activism in the United States.* New York: Oxford University Press, 2005.

Espirutu, Yen Le. *Asian American Panethnicity: Bridging Institutions and Identities.* Philadelphia: Temple University Press, 1992.

Faderman, Lillian, with Ghia Xiong, *I Begin My Life All Over: The Hmong and the American Immigrant Experience.* Boston: Beacon Press, 1998.

Fadiman, Anne. *The Spirit Catches You and You Fall Down: A Hmong Child, Her American Doctors and the Collision of Two Cultures*. New York: Farrar, Strauss and Giroux, 1997.

Fasenfest, David, Jason Booza, and Kurt Metzger. *Living Together: A New Look at Racial and Ethnic Integration in Metropolitan Neighborhoods*. Washington, DC: Brookings Institution, 2004.

Foley, Michael. *Religion and the New Immigrants: How Faith Communities Form Our Newest Citizens*. New York: Oxford University Press, 2007.

Foner, Nancy. *In a New Land: A Comparative View of Immigration*. New York: New York University Press, 2005.

———. *New Immigrants in New York*, Second Edition. New York: Columbia University Press, 2001.

Foner, Nancy, and George Fredrickson, ed. *Not Just Black and White: Historical and Contemporary Perspectives on Immigration, Race, and Ethnicity in the United States*. New York: Russell Sage Foundation, 2004.

Foner, Nancy, Ruben Rumbaut, and Steven Gold, ed. *Immigration Research for a New Century, Multidisciplinary Perspectives*. New York: Russell Sage Foundation, 2000.

Fong, Timothy. *The Contemporary Asian America Community: Beyond the Model Minority*, Third Edition. Upper Saddle River, NJ: Prentice Hall, 2007.

———. *The First Suburban Chinatown: The Remaking of Monterey Park, California*. Philadelphia: Temple University Press, 1994.

Freeman, James. *Hearts of Sorrow: Vietnamese American Lives*. Stanford, CA: Stanford University Press, 1991.

Fry, Brian. *Responding to Immigration: Perceptions of Promise and Threat*. New York: LFB Scholarly Publishing, 2001.

Fuchs, Lawrence. *The American Kaleidoscope: Race, Ethnicity and the Civic Culture*. Middletown, CT: Wesleyan University Press, 1990.

Gabbacia, Donna, and Vicki Ruiz, ed. *American Dreaming, Global Realities: Rethinking U.S. Immigration History*. Urbana-Champaign, IL: University of Illinois Press, 2006.

Gann, L. H., and Peter Duignan. *The Hispanics in the United States: A History*. Boulder, CO: Westview Press, 1986.

Garcia, Cristina. *Dreaming in Cuban*. New York: Ballantine Books, 1992.

Garcia, John. "Political Integration of Mexican Immigrants: Exploration into the Naturalization Process." *International Migration Review* 15 (1981): 608–625.

Garcia, Maria. *Havana USA: Cuban Exiles and Cuban Americans in South Florida, 1959–1994*. Berkeley, CA: University of California Press, 1996.

Gibson, Margaret. *Accommodation Without Assimilation: Sikh Immigrants in an American High School*. Ithaca, NY: Cornell University Press, 1989.

Gibson, Margaret, and John Ogbu. *Minority Status and Schooling: A Comparative Study of Immigrant and Involuntary Minorities*. New York: Garland, 1991.

Gjerde, Jon, ed. *Major Problems in American Immigration and Ethnic History*. Boston: Houghton Mifflin Company, 1998.

Glazer, Nathan. *Clamor at the Gates: The New American Immigration*. Ithaca, NY: ICS Press, 1985.

Gold, Steven. *Refugee Communities: A Comparative Field of Study*. Newbury Park, CA: Sage, 1992.

————. "Refugees and Small Business: The Case of Soviet Jews and Vietnamese." *Ethnic and Racial Studies* 11 (November 1988), 411–438.

Gozzini, Giovanni. "The Global System of International Migrations, 1900 and 2000: A Comparative Approach," *Journal of Global History* 1 (2006): 321–341.

Grasmuck, Sherri, and Patricia Pessar. *Between Two Islands: Dominican International Migration*. Berkeley, CA: University of California Press, 1991.

Grenier, Guillermo, and Lisandro Perez. *The Legacy of Exile: Cubans in the United States*. Boston: Allyn and Bacon, 2002.

Guarneri, Carl. *America in the World: United States History in Global Context*. Boston: McGraw Hill, 2007.

Gungwu, Wang, ed. *Global History and Migrations*. Boulder, CO: Westview, 1997.

Gutierrez, David. *Walls and Mirrors: Mexican Immigrants, Mexican Americans and the Politics of Ethnicity*. Berkeley, CA: University of California Press, 1995.

Haddad, Yvonne Yazbeck, and John Esposito, ed. *Muslims on the Americanization Path?* New York: Oxford University Press, 2000.

Haines, David, ed. *Refugees as Immigrants: Cambodians, Laotians and Vietnamese in America*. Totowa, NJ: Rowman and Littlefield, 1989.

————. *Refugees in the United States: A Reference Handbook*. Westport, CT: Greenwood Press, 1985.

Hakuta, Kenji. *Mirror of Language: The Debate on Bilingualism*. New York: Basic Books, 1986.

Halter, Marilyn. *New Migrants in the Market Place: Boston's Ethnic Entrepreneurs*. Amherst, MA: University of Massachusetts Press, 1995.

Harris, Nigel. *The New Untouchables: Immigration and the New World Worker*. London: I.B. Tauris, 1995.

Hatton, Timothy, and Jeffrey Williamson. *The Age of Mass Migration: Causes and Economic Impact*. New York: Oxford University Press, 1998.

Hegi, Ursula. *Tearing the Silence: On Being German in America*. New York: Simon & Schuster, 1997.

Hein, Jeremy. *From Vietnam, Laos, and Cambodia: A Refugee Experience in the United States*. New York: Twayne Publishers, 1995.

Hing, Bill Ong. *Making and Remaking Asian Americans through Immigration Policy, 1850–1990*. Stanford, CA: Stanford University Press, 1993.

Hinnels, John, ed. *A New Handbook of Living Religions*. New Edition. New York: Penguin Books, 1997.

————. *Dictionary of Religions*. Expanded New Edition. New York: Penguin Books, 1997.

Hirschman, Charles. "The Role of Religion in the Origins and Adaptation of Immigrant Groups in the United States." *International Migration Review* 38 (Fall 2004): 1206–1233.

Hoerder, Dirk. *Cultures in Contact: World Migrations in the Second Millennium*. Durham, NC: Duke University Press, 2002.

Hoffman, Eva. *Lost in Translation: A Life in a New Language*. New York: Penguin Books, 1990.

Hondagneu-Sotelo, Pierette. *Gendered Transitions: Mexican Experiences of Immigration*. Berkeley, CA: University of California Press, 1994.

Huntington, Samuel. *The Clash of Civilizations and the Remaking of World Order*. New York: Touchstone Books, 1997.

———. *Who Are We? The Challenges to America's National Identity.* New York: Simon and Schuster, 2004.

Ilsoo, Kim. *New Urban Immigrants: The Korean Community in New York.* Princeton, NJ: Princeton University Press, 1981.

Jacoby, Tamar, ed. *Reinventing the New Melting Pot: The New Immigrants and What It Means to Be an American.* New York: Basic Books, 2004.

Jasso, Guillermina, and Mark Rosenzweig. *The New Chosen People: Immigrants in the United States.* New York: Russell Sage Foundation, 1990.

Jencks, Christopher. *Rethinking Social Policy: Race, Poverty, and the Underclass.* Cambridge, MA: Harvard University Press, 1992.

Jensen, Joan. *Passage from India: Asian Indian Immigrants in North America.* New Haven, CT: Yale University Press, 1988.

Jones, Garreth, and Dennis Rodgers. *Youth Violence in Latin America: Gangs and Juvenile Justice in Perspective.* New York: Palgrave Macmillan, 2008.

Jones, Maldwyn. *American Immigration*, Second Edition. Chicago: University of Chicago Press, 1992.

Juss, Satvinder. *International Migration and Global Justice.* Aldershot, VT: Ashgate Publishing, 2006.

Kasinitz, Philip. *Caribbean New York: Black Immigrants and the Politics of Race.* Ithaca, NY: Cornell University Press, 1992.

Kasinitz, Philip, John Mollenkopf, Mary Waters, and Jennifer Holdaway. *Inheriting the City: The Children of Immigrants Come of Age.* New York: Russell Sage Foundation, 2008.

Kayyali, Randa. *The Arab Americans.* Westport, CT: Greenwood Publishing, 2005.

Kenney, David Ngarni, and Philip Schrag. *Asylum Denied: A Refugee's Struggle for Safety.* Berkeley, CA: University of California Press, 2008.

Khandelwal, Madhulika. *Becoming American, Being Indian: An Immigrant Community in New York City.* Ithaca, NY: Cornell University Press, 2002.

Kibria, Nazil. *Family Tightrope: The Changing Lives of Vietnamese Americans.* Princeton, NJ: Princeton University Press, 1993.

Kim, Elaine, and Eui Young Yu. *East to America: Korean American Life Stories.* New York: New Press, 1996.

Kingma, Mireille. *Nurses on the Move: Migration and the Global Health Care Economy.* Ithaca, NY: ILR Press, 2006.

Kitano, Harry, and Roger Daniels. *Asian Americans: Emerging Minorities*, Third Edition. Upper Saddle River, NJ: Prentice Hall, 2000.

Koltyk, Jo Ann. *New Pioneers in the Heartland: Hmong Life in Wisconsin.* Boston: Allyn and Bacon, 1997.

Koser, Khalid. *International Migration: A Very Short Introduction.* New York: Oxford University Press, 2007.

Krikorian, Mark. *The New Case against Immigration: Both Legal and Illegal.* New York: Sentinel, 2008.

Kroes, Rob. *Them and Us: Questions of Citizenship in a Globalizing World.* Urbana–Champaign, IL: University of Illinois Press, 2000.

Kwon, Okyun. *Buddhist and Protestant Korean Immigrants: Religious Beliefs and Socioeconomic Aspects of Life.* New York: LFB Scholarly Publishing, 2004.

Kwong, Peter. *Forbidden Workers: Illegal Chinese Immigrants and American Labor.* New York: New Press, 1999.

———. *The New Chinatown*, Revised Edition. New York: Hill and Wang, 1996.

Laguerre, Michel. *American Odyssey: Haitians in New York City.* Ithaca, NY: Cornell University Press, 1984.

Lehrer, Warren, and Judith Sloan. *Crossing the Boulevard: Strangers, Neighbors, Aliens in a New America.* New York: Norton, 2003.

Leonard, Karen Isaksen. *The South Asian Americans.* Westport, CT: Greenwood Press, 1997.

Levitt, Peggy. *Good Needs No Passport: Immigrants and the Changing American Religious Landscape.* New York: New Press, 2007.

———. *The Transnational Villagers.* Berkeley, CA: University of California Press, 2001.

Levitt, Peggy, and Mary Waters. Editors. *The Changing Face of Home: The Transnational Lives of the Second Generation.* New York: Russell Sage Foundation, 2006.

Light, Ivan, and Edna Bonacich. *Immigrant Entrepreneurs: Koreans in Los Angeles, 1965–1982.* Berkeley, CA: University of California Press, 1988.

Light, Ivan, and Steven Gold. *Ethnic Economies.* San Francisco: Academic Press, 2000.

Loucky, James, Jeanne Armstrong, and Larry Estrada. Editors. *Immigration in America Today: An Encyclopedia.* Westport, CT: Greenwood Press, 2006.

Mahler, Sarah. *American Dreaming: Immigrant Life at the Margins.* Princeton, NJ: University of Princeton Press, 1995.

Mangiafico, Luciano. *Contemporary American Immigrants: Patterns of Filipino, Korean, and Chinese Settlement in the United States.* Westport, CT: Praeger Publisher, 1988.

Manning, Patrick, *Migration in World History.* New York: Routledge, 2005.

Maraire, J. Nozipo. *Zenzele: A Letter for my Daughter.* New York: Delta Book, 1996.

Margolis, Maxine. *Little Brazil: An Ethnography of Brazilian Immigrants in New York City.* Princeton, NJ: Princeton University Press, 1994.

Martinez, Ruben. *Crossing Over: A Mexican Family on the Migrant Trail.* New York: Picador, 2002.

———. *The New Americans: Seven Families' Journey to America*, New Edition. New York: New Press, 2005.

———. *The Other Side: Notes from the New L.A., Mexico City and Beyond.* New York: Vintage, 1993.

Massey, Douglas, ed. *New Faces in New Places: The Changing Geography of American Immigration.* New York: Russell Sage Foundation, 2008.

Massey, Douglas, Joaquin Arango, Graeme Hugo, Ali Kouaouci, Adela Pellegrino, and J. Edward Taylor. *Worlds in Motion: Understanding International Migration at the End of the Millennium.* New York: Oxford University Press, 1998.

Massey, Douglas, Jorge Durand, and Nolan Malone. *Beyond Smoke and Mirrors: Mexican Immigration in an Era of Economic Integration.* New York: Russell Sage Foundation, 2003.

McKeown, Adam. "Global Migration, 1846–1940." *Journal of World History* 15 (2004): 155–189.

Menjiva, Cecilia. *Fragmented Ties: Salvadoran Immigrant Networks in America.* Berkeley, CA: University of California Press, 2000.

Millard, Ann, and Jorge Chapa. *Apple Pie and Enchiladas: Latino Newcomers in the Rural Midwest.* Austin, TX: University of Texas Press, 2004.

Miller, Jake. *The Plight of Haitian Refugees.* Westport, CT: Praeger, 1984.

Millman, Joel. *The Other Americans: How Immigrants Renew Our Country, Our Economy, and Our Values*. New York: Viking, 1997.

Min, Pyong Gap, ed. *Asian Americans: Contemporary Trends and Issues*, Second Edition. Thousand Oaks, CA: Sage, 2005.

Moses, Jonathon. *International Migration: Globalization's Final Frontier*. London: Zed Books, 2006.

Naff, Alixa. *The Arab Americans*. New York: Chelsea House Publications, 1998.

Occhiogrosso, Peter. *The Joy of Sects: A Spirited Guide to the World's Religious Traditions*. New York: Doubleday, 1994.

Ong, Paul, Edna Bonacich, and Lucie Cheng. *The New Asian Immigration in Los Angeles and Global Restructuring*. Philadelphia: Temple University Press, 1994.

Ono, Kent, and John Sloop, *Shifting Borders: Rhetoric, Immigration, and California's Proposition 187*. Philadelphia: Temple University Press, 2002.

Orfalea, Gregory. *Before the Flames: A Quest for the History of Arab Americans*. Austin, TX: University of Texas Press, 1988.

Pho, Tuyet-Lan, Jeffrey Gerson, and Sylvia Cowan, ed. *Southeast Asian Refugees and Immigrants in the Mill City*. Burlington, VT: University of Vermont Press, 2007.

Pipes, Daniel. *Muslim Immigrants in the United States*. Washington, DC: Center for Immigration Study, 2002.

Portes, Alejandro. "Immigration Theory for a New Century: Some Problems and Opportunities." *International Migration Review* 31 (Winter 1997): 799–825.

———, ed. *The Economic Sociology of Immigration*. New York: Russell Sage Foundation, 1995.

Portes, Alejandro, and Alex Stepick. *City on the Edge: The Transformation of Miami*. Berkeley, CA: University of California Press, 1994.

Portes, Alejandro, and Robert Back, *Latin Journey: Cuban and Mexican Immigrants in the United States*. Berkeley, CA: University of California Press, 1985.

Portes, Alejandro, and Ruben Rumbaut. *Immigrant America: A Portrait*, Third Edition. Berkeley, CA: University of California Press, 2006.

———. *Legacies: The Story of the Immigrant Second Generation*. Berkeley, CA: University of California Press, 2001.

Potts, Lydia. *The World Labour Market: A History of Migration*. London: Zed Books, 1990.

Priblisky, Jason. *La Chulla Vida: Gender, Migration, and the Family in Andean Ecuador and New York City*. Syracuse, NY: Syracuse University Press, 2007.

Price, Marie, and Lisa Benton Short, ed. *Migrants to the Metropolis: The Rise of Immigrant Gateway Cities*. Syracuse, NY: Syracuse University Press, 2008.

Ramakrishan, S. Karthick. *Democracy in Immigrant America: Changing Demographics and Political Participation*. Stanford, CA: Stanford University Press, 2005.

Rangaswamy, Padma. *Namaste America: Indian Immigrants in an American Metropolis*. University Park, PA: Pennsylvania State University Press, 2000.

Read, Jen'nan Ghazal. *Culture, Class, and Work among Arab-American Women*. New York: LFB Scholarly Publishing, 2004.

Reimers, David. *Still the Golden Door: The Third World Comes to America*, Second Edition. New York: Columbia University Press, 1992.

Rodriguez, Richard. *Days of Obligation: An Argument with My Mexican Father*. New York: Viking, 1992.

Rumbaut, Ruben, and Alejandro Portes. *Ethnicities: Children of Immigrants in America*. Berkeley, CA: University of California Press, 2001.

Rutledge, Paul. *The Vietnamese Experience in America*. Bloomington, IN: Indiana University Press, 1992.

Santoli, Al. *New Americans: An Oral History*. New York: Viking, 1988.

Sassen, Saskia. *The Mobility of Labor and Capital: A Study in International Investment and Labor Flow*. New York: Cambridge University Press, 1988.

Scanlan, John. *Calculated Kindness: Refugees and America's Half-Open Door, 1945 to the Present*. New York: New Press, 1986.

Scheffer, Gabriel, ed. *Modern Diasporas in International Politics*, Houndsmill, England: Palgrave Macmillan, 1986.

Shokeid, Moshe. *Children of Circumstances: Israeli Immigrants in New York*. Ithaca, NY: Cornell University Press, 1988.

Simon, Julian. *The Economic Consequences of Immigration*. Cambride, MA: Blackwell, 1989.

Skinner, E. Benjamin. *A Crime So Monstrous: Face-to-Face with Modern Slavery*. New York: Free Press, 2008.

Smith, James, and Barry Edmonston. *The Immigration Debate: Studies on the Economic, Demographic, and Fiscal Impacts of Immigration*. Washington, DC: National Academy Press, 1998.

Smith, Tom. "Religious Diversity in America: The Emergence of Muslims, Buddhists, Hindus, and Others." *Journal of the Scientific Study of Religion* 41, no. 3 (2002): 577–585.

Smith-Hefner, Nancy. *Khmer Americans: Identity and Moral Education in a Diasporic Community*. Berkeley, CA: University of California Press, 1999.

Sowell, Thomas. *Migrations and Cultures: A World View*. New York: Basic Books, 1996.

Spellman, William. *The Global Community: Migration and the Making of the Modern World*. Stroud, UK: Sutton Publishing, 2002.

Stalker, Peter. *Workers Without Frontiers: The Impact of Globalization on International Migration*. Boulder, CO: Lynne Rienner, 2000.

Stavans, Ilan, ed. *Immigration*. Westport, CT: Greenwood Press, 2008.

Steger, Manfred. *Globalization: A Very Short Introduction*. New York: Oxford University Press, 2003.

Stepick, Alex. *Pride Against Prejudice: Haitians in the United States*. Boston: Allyn and Bacon, 1998.

Stout, Robert Joe. *Why Immigrants Come to America: Bracheros, Indocumentados, and the Migra*. Westport, CT: Praeger, 2007.

Stowell, Jacob. *Immigration and Crime: The Effects of Immigration on Criminal Behavior*. New York: LFB Scholarly Publishing, 2007.

Strand, Paul, and Woodrow Jones Jr. *Indochinese Refugees in America: Problems of Adaptation and Assimilation*. Durham, NC: Duke University Press, 1985.

Suarez-Orozco, Marcelo. *Central American Refugees and U.S. High Schools: A Psychosocial Study of Motivation and Achievement*. Palo Alto, CA: Stanford University Press, 1989.

———. *Crossings: Mexican Immigration in Interdisciplinary Perspectives*. Cambridge, MA: David Rockefeller Center for Latin American Studies, Harvard University, 1998.

Suarez-Orozco, Marcelo, and Carola Suarez-Orozco. *Children of Immigration*. Cambridge, MA: Harvard University Press, 2001.

Suarez-Orozco, Marcelo, Carola Suarez-Orozco, and Irina Todorova. *Learning in a New Land: Immigrant Students in American Society.* Cambridge, MA: Belknap Press, 2008.

Suleiman, Michael. *Arabs in America: Building a New Future*. Philadelphia: Temple University, 2000.

Takaki, Ronald. *A Different Mirror: A History of Multicultural America*. Boston: Back Bay, 1993.

———. *Strangers from a Different Shore: A History of Asian Americans*, Second Edition. Boston: Back Bay, 1998.

Teitlebaum, Michael, and Myron Weiner. *Threatened Peoples, Threatened Borders: World Migration and U.S. Policy.* New York: Norton, 1995.

Thernstrom, Stephan, ed. *Harvard Encyclopedia of American Ethnic Groups*. Cambridge, MA: Harvard University Press, 1981.

Toro-Morn, Maura, and Marixsa Alicia. Editors. *Migration and Immigration: A Global View.* Westport, CT: Greenwood Press, 2004.

Trager, Lillian. *Migration and Economy: Global and Local Dynamics*. New York: Alta Mira Press, 2005.

Ueda, Reed. *Postwar Immigrant America: A Social History.* Boston: Bedford/St. Martin's, 1994.

Ungar, Sanford. *Fresh Blood: The New American Immigrants*. New York: Simon Schuster, 1995.

Vega, William, and Ruben Rumbaut. "Ethnic Minorities and Mental Health." *Annual Review of Sociology* 17 (1991): 351–383.

Waldinger, Roger. *Still the Promised City? African-Americans and New Immigrants in Postindustrial New York*. Cambridge MA: Harvard University Press, 1996.

———, ed. *Strangers at the Gates: New Immigrants in Urban America*. Berkeley, CA: University of California Press, 2001.

Waldinger, Roger, and Michael I. Lichter. *How the Other Half Works: Immigration and the Social Organization of Labor*. Berkeley, CA: University of California Press, 2003.

Warner, Stephen, and Judith Wittner, ed. *Gatherings in Diaspora: Religious Communities and the New Immigration*. Philadelphia: Temple University Press, 1998.

Waters, Mary. *Black Identities: West Indian Immigrant Dreams and American Realities*. New York: Russell Sage Foundation, 1999.

Waters, Mary, and Reed Ueda. *The New Americans: A Guide to Immigration Since 1965*. Cambridge, MA: Harvard University Press, 2007.

Welaratna, Usha. *Beyond the Killing Fields: Voices of Nine Cambodian Survivors in America*. Stanford, CA: Stanford University Press, 1994.

Welch, Michael. *Scapegoats of September 11: Hate Crimes and State Crimes in the War on Terror*. New Brunswick, NJ: Rutgers University Press, 2006.

Williamson, Jr., Chilton, ed. *Immigration and the American Future*. Rockford, IL: Chronicle Press and the Rockford Institute, 2007.

Yans-McLaughlin, Virginia, ed. *Immigration Reconsidered: History, Sociology, and Politics*. New York: Oxford University Press, 1990.

Zhang, Sheldon. *Smuggling and Trafficking in Human Beings: All Roads Lead to America*. Westport, CT: Praeger, 2007.

Zhou, Min, and Carl Bankston. *Growing Up American: How Vietnamese Children Adapt to Life in the United States.* New York: Russell Sage Foundation, 1998.

Zolberg, Aristide. *A Nation by Design: Immigration Policy in the Fashioning of America.* Cambridge, MA: Harvard University Press, 2006.

———. "The Next Waves: Migration Theory for a Changing World." *International Migration Review* 23 (Fall 1989): 403–430.

Zolberg, Aristide, and Peter Benda, ed. *Global Migrants, Global Refugees: Problems and Solutions.* New York: Berghahn Books, 2001.

Zolberg, Aristide, Astri Suhrke, and Sergio Aguayo. *Escape from Violence: Conflict and the Refugee Crisis in the Developing World.* New York: Oxford University Press, 1989.

———. "International Factors in the Formation of Refugee Movements." *International Migration Review* 20 (Summer 1986): 151–169.

Zuniga, Victor, and Ruben Hernandez-Leon, ed. *New Destinations: Mexican Immigration in the United States.* New York: Russell Sage Foundation, 2006.

INDEX

About the Author

CHRISTOPH STROBEL is Assistant Professor of History at the University of Massachusetts Lowell. His research focuses on international immigration, comparative race/ethnicity, and Native American history. He is the author of *The Testing Grounds of Modern Empire* (2008) and coauthor, with Alice Nash, of *Daily Life of Native Americans from Post-Columbian through Nineteenth-Century America* (Greenwood 2006).